Companion Animals in Soci

Council for Science and Society:
Reports of Working Parties also
published by Oxford University Press

Human Procreation: Ethical Aspects
    of the New Techniques
UK Military R&D

Companion Animals in Society

Report of a Working Party
Council for Science and Society

Oxford New York Tokyo
OXFORD UNIVERSITY PRESS
1988

Oxford University Press, Walton Street, Oxford OX2 6DP

Oxford New York Toronto
Delhi Bombay Calcutta Madras Karachi
Petaling Jaya Singapore Hong Kong Tokyo
Nairobi Dar es Salaam Cape Town
Melbourne Auckland

and associated companies in
Berlin Ibadan

Oxford is a trade mark of Oxford University Press

Published in the United States
by Oxford University Press, New York

British Library Cataloguing in Publication Data
Companion animals in society : report of
a working party.
1. Man. Relationships with pets
2. Pets. relationships with man
I. Council for Science and Society
304.2
ISBN 0-19-857697-8

Library of Congress Cataloging-in-Publication Data
Companion animals in society : report of a working party, Council for
Science and Society.
Bibliography:
1. Pets—Great Britain.   2. Pets—Social aspects—Great Britain.
3. Pets—Moral and ethical aspects—Great Britain.   4. Pet
owners—Great Britain.   I. Council for Science and Society.
SF411.5.C66   1988   636.08'87—dc19   88-6599
ISBN 0-19-857697-8 (pbk.)

Set by CentraCet, Cambridge
Printed in Great Britain
at the University Printing House, Oxford
by David Stanford,
Printer to the University

About the Council

The Council for Science and Society, a registered charity, was formed in 1973 with the object of 'promoting the study of, and research into, the social effects of science and technology, and of disseminating the results thereof to the public'.

The Council's primary task is to stimulate informed public discussion in the field of 'the social responsibility of the scientist'. It seeks to identify developments in science and technology whose social consequences lie just over the horizon, where no full-scale debate has yet begun. Experience shows that intensive analysis of the present (and probable future) 'state of the art', and of the foreseeable social consequences, can suggest a range of possible responses to those who will sooner or later have to take the necessary decisions. The Council carries out this task in a number of different ways, including the organization of conferences, seminars, and colloquia.

Major studies are conducted by *ad hoc* working parties, composed – like the Council itself – of experts in the respective fields together with lawyers, philosophers, and others who can bring a wide range of skills and experience to bear on the subject. The results of these studies are published in the form of reports such as this one. It is the Council's hope that these will help others to work out the most appropriate solutions to these problems in the course of responsible public debate, conducted at leisure on the best information available, rather than by the hurried, ill-informed, and ill-considered process which is apt to occur if the community does not become aware of a problem until it is too late.

The Council is grateful to the Trustees of the Esmée Fairbairn Trust, the Nuffield Foundation, and the Wates Foundation for financial support.

The Council welcomes all suggestions of further subjects for study.

COUNCIL FOR SCIENCE AND SOCIETY,
3/4 St Andrews Hill,
London EC4V 5BY
Tel: 01-236-6723

Council Members

Membership of the Working Party

Professor Lawson Soulsby Chairman
Professor of Animal Pathology and Head of Department of Clinical Veterinary Medicine, University of Cambridge

Dr James Serpell Rapporteur
Director, Companion Animal Research Group, University of Cambridge

Professor Patrick Bateson, FRS
Professor of Animal Behaviour, Sub-Department of Animal Behaviour, Department of Zoology, and Professor of Ethology, University of Cambridge

Professor Gordon Dunstan
Emeritus Professor of Moral and Social Theology, University of London. Honorary Research Fellow, University of Exeter.

Professor John Humphrey, FRS*
Emeritus Professor of Immunology, Royal Post-Graduate Medical School, University of London

Mr Peter Mann
Principal Veterinary Officer, People's Dispensary for Sick Animals

Mr N. King
Chairman, British Veterinary Association Animal Welfare Foundation

Dr Martin Richards
Department of Paediatrics and Social and Political Sciences Committee, University of Cambridge

Dr Alan Walker
Chairman, Wood Green Animal Shelter

Secretary

Barbara Farah

---

* Professor Humphrey died on 25 December 1987

Foreword

Lawson Soulsby, *Chairman of the Working Party on Companion Animals*
John Ziman, *Chairman of the Council for Science and Society*

This is the first comprehensive evaluation of companion animals in society. It reveals the complexity of the situation and explores the various ramifications of companion animal ownership. How should we define a 'companion animal'? This is more difficult than it might first appear, since companionship bonds may be developed with many species that would not immediately be considered as pets – for example thoroughbred horses and racing pigeons. It is necessary to recognize that companion animals can play many different roles, each of which needs to be examined in some depth.

A brief history of pet-keeping through the ages shows that the perception of animals has changed considerably over the centuries. Present-day attitudes demonstrate the strong attachment and empathy that many people feel towards their animal companions. This is borne out nationally by the millions of households in the UK that keep one or more cats or dogs, and by the range of other species that are also kept as companion animals.

The companion animal 'industry' contributes substantially to the national economy, through the sale of pets, pet food and accessories, and in the form of veterinary care.

Companion animals provide many benefits which are difficult to quantify in monetary terms, but which have important implications for the health and welfare of humans. Nevertheless, pet ownership creates problems, which often culminate in abandonment. Other, less obvious, problems are those of behaviour, physical and genetic mutilations for cosmetic or fad purposes and, of course, the dangers of disease transmission, causation of accidents, and damage. The legal aspects of companion animal ownership are complex and contained in a multitude of regulations. A number of ethical issues need to be considered, including the issue of animal rights.

It is evident that the keeping of companion animals in the UK is a widespread and entrenched feature of life. It satisfies human interests and is not ordinarily contrary to the social or public interest. A major purpose of this study will be to inform the public of the responsibilities associated with the keeping of pets.

The final realization of this report is due to the combined efforts of a number of people. We are particularly grateful for the outstanding work of our rapporteur, Dr James Serpell, who prepared and skilfully assembled many diverse items into a comprehensive, coherent, and highly readable text. James

Serpell gratefully acknowledges that his efforts were assisted by the enthusiastic advice and expert contributions of individual members of the Working Party as well as by the Council's then Executive Secretary, Barbara Farah.

This project would not have come to fruition without specific financial help. The Council gratefully acknowledges the generous grants received from the Blue Cross Animals' Hospital, British Petroleum, the Guide Dogs for the Blind Association, the People's Dispensary for Sick Animals, and Spillers Foods.

Acknowledgements

The Working Party wishes to thank the following persons and organizations for their assistance in the preparation of the Report:

Mr W. S. Ellis, Chairman, The Birmingham Dogs' Home
Mr P. Hannon, Secretary, The Blue Cross
Mr A. C. Crook, General Secretary/Treasurer, The Budgerigar Society
Mr B. Byles, Editor, Cage and Aviary Birds
Group Cpt. H. E. Boothby, Director, The Cats' Protection League
Mr W. M. W. Taylor, Manager, The Dogs' Home Battersea
Mrs E. Svendson and Mr. B. H. Bagnell, The Donkey Sanctuary
Mr R. K. Connell, Manager, The Edinburgh Dog and Cat Home
Mr R. Batty, Managing Editor, Fur and Feather
Mr D. R. S. Fraser, Manager, The Glasgow and West of Scotland Dog and Cat Home
Mrs L. Pring, Governing Council of the Cat Fancy
Ms H. Pane, Secretary, Joint Advisory Committee on Pets in Society
Mr W. B. Edmond, Asst. Secretary and **Miss T. Slowik**, Librarian, The Kennel Club
Mr C. R. de la Wyche, Secretary, Manchester and District Home for Lost Dogs
Mrs C. M. Baldwin, Secretary, The National Canine Defence League
Miss E. Archer, Secretary, The Pet Food Manufacturers Association
Ms P. Bloom, Managing Director and **Mr J. Brownlee**, General Manager, Pet Plan Ltd.
Mr R. Stonebridge, Editor, Pet Product Marketing
Mr M. Colle, Secretary, Pet Trade and Industry Association
Mrs J. Todd, Superintendent, Plymouth & District Dogs' and Cats' Home Charity
Mr D. B. Wilkins, Chief Veterinary Officer, Royal Society for the Prevention of Cruelty to Animals
Mrs S. Zabawa, Freelance Journalist
Dr V. O'Farrell, Royal (Dick) School of Veterinary Studies, Edinburgh
Mrs L. Scott Ordish, PRO DOGS National Charity
Mr Graham Fuller, The Wood Green Animal Shelter
Prof Leo K. Bustad, The Delta Society, USA
Mr M. J. R. Stockman
The Rt. Hon. Alfred Morris, MP
The Hon. Mrs Moyra Williams, Equine Behaviour Study Circle

Mr P. J. N. Pinsent
Mr G. R. Walmsley and Mr K. Bannister, HM Prison Service
Mr R. Sankey, Tropical Marine Centre
Mr J. Dawes
Dr J. Barzdo, IUCN Wildlife Trade Monitoring Unit, Cambridge
Mr K. Barraclough
Mrs M. Cooper
Euromonitor Publications
Mintel Market Intelligence
BBC Television 'That's Life' Programme
The Union of Communication Workers
The Society for Companion Animal Studies
The British Horse Society

Contents

1 Introduction

The relationship between animals and man is one of antiquity. From the earliest cultures animals have played a dominant role in the provision of motive power for agriculture, in the conversion of cellulose to meat and milk, and as the focus of religious beliefs and worship. Many of these roles remain important today, especially in developing countries, but in the increasingly urban society of the developed world the role of animals has changed considerably. Animals are interwoven into the complex fabric of post-industrial civilization and they continue to serve mankind in a multitude of different roles. They remain an essential part of intensive food and fibre production, they are widely used for sport, recreation, and performance, and they are employed in scientific experiments − a contentious area. They also serve less direct roles by, for example, contributing to the environment as component parts of ecological systems, and as sentinels of the abuse of the environment by modern society. But perhaps the role most commonly identified for animals nowadays is that of companionship.

This report deals specifically with the role of companion animals in society but, nevertheless, the subject is complex and tends to impinge on some of the broader roles of animals already described. It has been necessary to define what is meant by the term 'companion animals'. While this may be relatively straightforward for dogs and cats, it is less clear for other species, such as horses, and decidedly unclear for animals such as fish, molluscs, insects, and the like. Further, the reason for owning a companion animal may not be for companionship alone, but for protection, status, or as compensation for emotional loss. The report goes on to discuss the extent of keeping companion animals, and the benefits and problems associated with their ownership. Related issues are the supply, servicing, and cost of companion animals, legal responsibilities, unwanted animals, and the ethical issues arising from our use of animals for this purpose.

Companion animals may be assumed to play an important role in our society, since more than twelve million pet dogs and cats are kept in the United Kingdom. Their direct contribution to human health and happiness is significant, and the service industry which supports them also contributes substantially to the economy of the nation. But these are only some of the issues which relate to companion animals and their owners, and the reader may be surprised to discover the overall breadth of the topic discussed in this report.

This is the first time that a detailed consideration of companion animals in society has been attempted. The report confirms the complexity of the subject, and the social, economic, legal, and ethical ramifications of keeping companion animals. In conclusion, it contains a number of recommendations which address major issues identified in the report.

2 What is a companion animal?

The decision to adopt the phrase *companion animals* (in preference to the more traditional term *pets*) in the title of this report was prompted by several factors. Until recently, any tame or domestic animal that did not appear to serve an obvious practical or economic function was often merely classified as a pet. The word therefore covers a multitude of quite different phenomena, depending on a person's motive for keeping an animal and the nature of his or her relationship with it. Cats and stick insects, for example, may be owned by the same individual for quite different reasons, yet both can be regarded as pets in a general sense. The apparent lack of utility implied by the word pet is also misleading, since it implies that what people derive from relationships with animals can only be described or understood in economic terms. But in the last ten or so years it has been established that some pets provide people with a variety of social and psychological benefits, and that the owners of these animals sometimes value them as highly as human friends or companions. It is also apparent, from the sheer extent of the phenomenon, that this companionship role of pets in Western society is now of greater importance than ever before.

People keep pets for many different reasons, and it is therefore useful, at the beginning of this report, to propose a system of classifying these animals that takes the various different motives into account. At the same time, it needs to be emphasized that the categories provided are neither exclusive nor definitive since a species or breed typical of one group may well turn up in others.

2.1 PETS AS ORNAMENTS

Since antiquity, animals and representations of animals have been used frequently for decorative purposes. For obvious reasons, brightly coloured and aesthetically pleasing species, such as exotic birds and aquarium fish, are most commonly employed in this role. In the seventeenth and eighteenth centuries the wealthy owners of stately homes imported peacocks and oriental pheasants to adorn their country estates. Caged or tethered songbirds were also concealed in garden foliage in order to enrich the air with melodious bird song (Tuan 1984). In many parts of southern Europe it is still customary to hang cages of canaries or wild songbirds outside shops and houses for the same purpose. In Britain, decorative aquaria containing freshwater or marine tropical fish are a familiar sight, both in private homes and in the reception areas of large hotels

3

and office blocks. Animals kept like this for decoration are seldom handled or named, and seem to occupy essentially the same role as potted palms and house plants.

2.2   PETS AS STATUS SYMBOLS

Animals have long been valued for symbolic reasons. In many tribal societies certain species are adopted as totems; emblems or insignia of particular clans and subgroups which are then used as the basis for structuring and organizing tribal loyalties and relationships. Vestiges of this tradition can be detected in medieval heraldry and in the modern use of regimental animal mascots. Rare, unusual, or exotic animals have also been used to symbolize power and affluence. Since Roman times, European monarchs and aristocrats have employed strange animals and private menageries as a means of advertising their elevated social status. To a lesser degree, pets are still used for the same purpose today. Unusual and expensive breeds of dog or cat, for example, may be owned as much for reasons of prestige as for anything else. Animals kept solely as status symbols are often admired and well looked after, but only as long as the image they project corresponds to the owner's expectations.

2.3   PETS AS PLAYTHINGS

Many so-called 'pets' are kept primarily for sporting, recreational, or playful purposes. Children who are too young to fully appreciate them are often provided with small animals, such as hamsters, goldfish, tadpoles, and terrapins, which serve as animated toys. As with most toys, enthusiasm is often temporary, and the animals are generally badly treated and short-lived. Among adults, horses and dogs often fulfil similar roles – for riding, hunting, racing, performing tricks, etc. – although the relationship with the owner is generally less ephemeral. People's attitudes to sporting and recreational pets are complex and hard to define. Some owners appear to derive satisfaction from the exercise of dominating and controlling the animal. Others stress the rewards of communicating with the animal and identifying with its physical skills and performance. During its prime, the recreational pet may be the object of considerable affection, but it may also be discarded or destroyed with few signs of emotion when it ceases to amuse.

2.4   PETS AS HOBBIES

Considerable overlap exists between this and the previous category, since many recreational activities involving animals are also hobbies. The category has therefore been created in order to accommodate the typical hobbyist who specializes in collecting and breeding particular species or groups of animals in much the same way that others collect stamps, coins, or vintage wines. Animal hobbyists often belong to clubs, societies or *fancies* of like-minded people which organize regular meeting or shows where the members can display the pride of their collections. In some cases, these shows are intensely competitive affairs with highly coveted prizes. There are huge numbers of such societies covering everything from dogs and cats to cage birds and ornamental fish (see §4.3). As with recreational pets, relationships between hobbyists and their charges are complex. Hobbyists are enthusiasts and they generally possess a considerable breadth of knowledge about their chosen group or species. The animals are generally well cared for, since this is synonymous with good husbandry, and they are often regarded with affection. Occasionally, they are viewed as merely a means to an end in the pursuit of competitive success or the prize-winning specimen.

2.5 PETS AS COMPANIONS

The crucial thing that defines a companion animal, and distinguishes it from other pets, is the nature of the relationship with the owner. An animal employed for decoration, status-signalling, recreation, or hobby is being used primarily as an object – the animal equivalent of a work of art, a Rolls Royce, a surfboard, or a collector's item. The companion animal, however, is typically perceived and treated as a subject; as a personality in its own right, irrespective of other considerations. With companion animals it is the relationship itself which is important to the owner. The animal's physical qualities may be irrelevant. With other kinds of pet, social interactions and relationships are often just a means to an end.

For obvious reasons, relationships with companion animals are similar to relationships with human companions. In many ways they are also as complex. No two human relationships are ever precisely identical, since each clearly depends on the individual character and expectations of those involved. The same is largely true of relationships with companion animals. Each will depend on the personality of the owner, and what he or she hopes to derive from the partnership, as well as on the individual and species characteristics of the animal. At the same time, just as it is possible to identify certain typical human relationships – for example friendships, parent–child, husband–wife, etc. – it is also possible to envisage various standard types of relationships with companion animals. All human–dog relationships, for example, share certain features in common which distinguish them from human–cat or human–horse relationships. Conversely, an individual dog may fulfil quite different roles for different members of the same family: one may perceive it as a child, another as a friend, another as a servant, and so on. As with human relationships, relationships with companion animals can be either good – mutually rewarding to both participants – or bad.

Referring to a species or a breed as a companion animal does not, of course, preclude its exploitation for other purposes. Many so-called 'companion animals' serve a variety of functions. A family dog, for instance, could, in theory, be valued simultaneously as a status object, a burglar alarm, an aid to recreation, and as a companion. Indeed, in some instances, for example in the case of working sheepdogs or racing greyhounds, the companionship role may be incidental and subordinate to other, more utilitarian functions. Virtually any kind of pet can serve as a companion animal, although dogs, cats and, to a lesser extent, horses, budgerigars, rabbits, and other small mammals are the species traditionally associated with this role.

Dogs and cats possess the distinction that they are among the few domestic species not requiring cages, fences, or tethers in order to enforce their association with people. This characteristic has undoubtedly enhanced their popularity as companions. Both species form durable social bonds with their owners, and cats, in addition, become strongly attached to particular locations. In the majority of social mammals, the formation of primary social attachments occurs most readily during relative short *sensitive periods* in early life. If the developing individual is exposed to contact with humans or other species during this period, it will tend to incorporate them into its social world. Conversely, if isolated from such contacts, it will tend to remain permanently shy. In dogs and cats, the sensitive period for socialization is relatively protracted, and this improves their capacity to form close bonds with individuals other than the mother or litter-mates.

Another reason why people find it necessary to cage some pets and not others is in order to control where the animal deposits its waste-products. Again, cats and dogs have the advantage that they are relatively easy to house-train. With birds and the majority of other mammalian pets, house-training is virtually impossible. Their physical size may also have contributed to the overwhelming success of dogs and cats as companions. They are large enough for people to be able to relate to them as recognizable individuals. And they are sufficiently small that they generally pose little in the way of a serious hazard or threat.

Perhaps the most important factor contributing to the popularity of dogs and cats as animal companions is their power of non-verbal expression. Both species possess a rich and unambiguous repertoire of postures, gestures, facial signals, and sounds which they use to communicate with their owners. Above all, many of these signals are interpreted by people as expressions of attachment and affection. The animal thus conveys to the owner a feeling of being valued and needed, and this sense of being needed is probably one of the greatest rewards of companion animal ownership (see §5.2). Because they are expressive, dogs and cats are also anthropomorphic. They are easy to personify and think of in human terms. Pet-owners are frequently guilty of misinterpreting or over-interpreting the behaviour of their animals as a result of such anthropomorphism but, nevertheless, their ability to relate to companion animals as human beings undoubtedly helps to intensify the relationship. In addition, pets cannot speak and, while obviously limiting the scope of the relationship, this also means that companion animals are incapable of lying to, deceiving, or criticizing their owners. In other words, they combine many of the benefits of human relationships with few of the threats (Serpell 1986).

Apart from livestock, companion animals are now by far the largest and the most influential category of domestic animals in modern society. For this reason they provide the primary focus of the present study.

2.6 PETS AS HELPERS

Although, strictly speaking, pets are seldom used for the performance of important economic or practical tasks, in practice the distinction between pets and working animals is often blurred. Working sheepdogs, for example, may be owned primarily for the purpose of herding livestock, and are sometimes viewed and treated by their owners with considerable detachment. Often, however, individual animals are regarded with great affection, and may be cherished by the owner long after they have ceased to be economically useful. Guide-dogs trained to assist visually impaired people occupy a similar position. Their primary role or *raison d'etre* is to enhance the owner's physical mobility. But often they are valued as much for the companionship they provide as they are for their practical assistance. Both of these examples illustrate the human tendency to form social bonds with tame or domestic animals. When attachments like these interfere with the effective economic exploitation of such species, they can be suppressed. Otherwise they tend to emerge as the natural outcome of close, cooperative interaction (Serpell 1986).

3 A history of companion animals

It is commonly assumed that the use of animals for companionship is a relatively modern Western phenomenon. In reality, this form of pet-keeping is of considerable antiquity and may pre-date the development of farming or the true domestication of animals. In many subsistence hunting and gathering and simple horticultural societies, young wild mammals and birds are captured, tamed, and kept as pets. These animals appear to serve little or no utilitarian purpose and, although they often belong to species that are regularly hunted for food, they are never, in the normal course of events, killed or eaten. Their owners devote considerable time and energy to their care, and often display remorse when they die. Women will even suckle young mammals at the breast alongside their own infants.

There is no direct means of establishing whether the hunting cultures of the late Stone Age kept wild animal pets in this way. But, since their overall lifestyle was essentially similar to that of their more recent counterparts, this is likely to have been the case. That man's earliest relationship with species such as the domestic dog was an affectionate one is also suggested by at least one important archaeological discovery. In 1978, at a late Palaeolithic site in northern Israel, a tomb was uncovered in which the remains of a human and a dog had been buried together roughly 12 000 years ago. Whoever presided over the original burial appears to have arranged the dead person's hand on the animal's shoulder, as if to emphasize the bonds that existed between these two individuals during life. Several archaeologists and anthropologists have also speculated that Stone Age pet-keeping provided the base from which animal domestication and husbandry subsequently evolved.

Reports of pet-keeping among aboriginal peoples date back to the earliest days of European colonialism. Explorers and missionaries who visited the New World during the sixteenth, seventeenth, and eighteenth centuries described the Indians keeping pet raccoons, monkeys, peccaries, tapirs, wolves, bears, moose, various small rodents, and innumerable species of wild birds for companionship. Although offered substantial payment, the Indians often refused to part with their pets, and sometimes became distraught with grief when the animals were forcibly taken away from them. The vast majority of these early accounts express amusement or astonishment at the degree of affection demonstrated by these people for their companion animals; a clear indication that in Europe at this time such profound attachments between

8

people and animals were rare or non-existent. Indeed, in England during the sixteenth and seventeenth centuries, pet-keeping among the general population seems to have been regarded with some suspicion, and it was even used, on occasions, as the basis for allegations of witchcraft. Many of the individuals who were brought to trial and executed in England for the crime of witchcraft were incriminated by the fact that they kept, and were seen to display affection for, one or more animal companions or 'familiars'.

The nobility at this time were largely immune to this degree of public censure, and many of them kept companion animals – chiefly birds and small lapdogs – in profusion. Nevertheless, their extravagant pet-keeping habits were sometimes the subject of caustic remarks by writers and commentators of the period. This association between pets and the aristocracy was part of a long historical tradition which dated back to the great civilizations of antiquity. The murals and papyri of ancient Egypt, for example, indicate that the Pharoahs and many of their high-ranking officials kept dogs, cats, and various tame wild animals for company. These animals were given personal names, treated royally, and evidently regarded with affection. The wealthier citizens of ancient Greece and Rome were also ardent pet-lovers, and classical literature abounds with sentimental eulogies to favourite dogs, birds, and horses. In China during the twelfth century AD pet dogs became an Imperial obsession. Pekinese or Lion Dogs were the principal objects of this infatuation, and at the height of their popularity during the eighteenth century Ch'ing dynasty these animals enjoyed a status unrivalled by any variety of pet before or since. Puppies were suckled at the breasts of Imperial wet-nurses; adults were given princely rank and were permanently attended by a retinue of palace eunuchs (Serpell 1986).

Pet-keeping never appears to have gained much favour outside the ruling classes in China. In Europe, however, toward the end of the seventeenth century, companion animal ownership began to spread downwards into the newly emergent urban middle-classes. This expansion of the pet population coincided with the so-called Age of Enlightenment, during which the anthropocentric and exploitative attitudes towards living creatures that had dominated medieval and Renaissance thought were gradually replaced by a growing sympathy and enthusiasm for animals and nature. It is probable that the close, affectionate relationships that existed between seventeenth and eighteenth century moralists and their pets played a part in bringing about this change of heart (Thomas 1983).

Within the last century the growth in popularity of companion animals has continued and accelerated, and this historical trend probably reflects demographic and social changes. Although companion animal ownership is clearly not just a product of material affluence, it is likely that rising standards of living over the last fifty or so years have helped to encourage the growth of Western pet populations. It is also possible that the decline in birth rate and family size over the same period has created a need for alternative outlets for parental nurturance and care. The discovery of artificial sources of power – steam, electricity, and petroleum – may also have made companion animals more attractive, by reducing the amount of day-to-day contact between people and working animals. Above all, changes in overall attitudes to animals seem to have been important. During the Middle Ages and Renaissance, the vast majority of people lived and worked in rural settings, and were daily involved with the management, exploitation, and slaughter of domestic animals. Animals were regarded as the servants or slaves of humanity, and sentimental concern or affection for animals was strongly discouraged. During the last three hundred years, however, the bulk of the population has moved into towns or cities, and perhaps only 2 to 3 per cent still work on the land or have any direct involvement with livestock production or slaughter. This shift from rural to urban life seems to have cultivated a less utilitarian and more sympathetic attitude to animals in general, and to pets in particular (Thomas 1983; Serpell 1986).

4 The extent and economic significance of the pet-keeping phenomenon

Although the British are reputedly a nation of animal lovers, they in fact rank fourth in the EEC – with Belgium, Italy, and the Irish Republic – in terms of the percentage of households owning at least one companion animal (European Pet Food Industry Federation 1987). This section examines the extent of the pet-keeping phenomenon in Britain, and considers its overall economic importance in commercial terms.

4.1 THE SUPPLY OF COMPANION ANIMALS

4.1.1 *Dogs*

Current UK statistics indicate a population of 6.3 million pet dogs, kept in roughly 5 million households (Pet Food Manufacturer's Association Profile 1987). In 1963 a population of 4.4 million was reported, suggesting an average annual increase of about 90 000 animals. Although the normal lifespan of the domestic dog is 12 to 14 years, accidents, disease, and deliberate euthanasia (putting to sleep) reduce the figure to an average of 10 years. It follows from this that at least 700 000 puppies a year are needed to maintain the population and continue the upward trend.

Roughly half the dogs in Britain are pure-bred and, of these, about half are registered as puppies by the British Kennel Club. Apart from a sharp decline during the early part of the Second World War, the numbers of puppies registered has risen fairly steadily from 58 799 in 1935 to 198 000 in 1986. Registered puppies command prices of up to £1000 or more depending on quality and rarity, but the average at present is about £120. Pure-bred but unregistered puppies of lesser quality sell for around £80. The 350 000 or so cross-bred puppies that escape destruction at birth or soon after tend to be either given away locally, sold by animal rescue societies for about £10 or, if particularly attractive, by pet shops for around £25. Based on these estimates, the total market value of commercial trade in pet dogs works out at about £40 million a year. Of this roughly £3 million is generated by the export of high quality animals that fetch greater than average prices.

The number of people actually employed full-time in dog breeding is small. A few large establishments, mostly in Wales and the south-west of England, keep substantial numbers of breeding animals and supply outlets in the cities. There are also a few hundred smaller kennels that breed quality stock, much of which is exported to provide a reasonable income. For the majority, however, dog breeding is a hobby combined with dog showing, and those involved barely, if ever, cover their outgoings. These costs often include the part-time employment of animal attendants. Many breeders also supplement their income by running boarding kennels. About 30 000 dog breeders have their names registered with the Kennel Club as protected 'affixes'. Dividing this number into the total market for pure-bred dogs, produces an average annual turnover of £1200 per breeder.

The ten most popular dog breeds registered with the Kennel Club in 1985 were: 1. German shepherd dogs (Alsatians); 2. Labrador retrievers; 3. Yorkshire terriers; 4. golden retrievers; 5. cavalier King Charles spaniels; 6. Dobermanns; 7. Rottweilers; 8. cocker spaniels; 9. English springer spaniels; and 10. Staffordshire bull terriers (*Kennel Gazette* April 1987). The trend since 1960 has been towards a substantial increase in the numbers of large guarding breeds – notably German shepherds, Dobermanns, and Rottweilers – and a reduction in the popularity of small dogs, such as toy and miniature poodles, corgis, and Pekinese.

4.1.2   *Cats*

Roughly 6.2 million cats are currently kept in 4.2 million homes. The number has grown from 4 million in 1963; a slightly more rapid increase than that recorded for dogs. Judging from the statistics, the increase can be largely attributed to individual households keeping more cats, rather than more households keeping cats. Although the cat's normal lifespan is about 15 years, it appears that cross-bred animals, which constitute 95 per cent of the population, live on average only five or six years owing to disease and heavy losses in road accidents. If this figure is correct, it follows that at least a million kittens are needed each year to replenish the population. The vast majority of these animals are acquired at little or no cost to the owner.

The 300 000 or so pure-bred cats in Britain tend to be more carefully protected, and may average about ten years of life. Pure-bred kittens are sold for about £50, although a small proportion of rare or high-quality individuals may fetch up to several hundred pounds. Assuming an average price of £60, the annual trade in pedigree cats probably only amounts to about £2 million. Even after the addition of a million cross-bred kittens, the total market is unlikely to exceed £5 million. A very few breeders of pedigree cats make an adequate income from their activities. For the great majority, cat breeding is even more of a hobby than dog-breeding, and as a source of full-time employment it can virtually be disregarded.

4.1.3   *Horses, ponies, and donkeys*

The British Horse Society estimates that there are roughly 500 000 horses and ponies in Britain, many of which are companion animals in the sense that they are kept primarily for companionship and recreation and, like dogs and cats, are often regarded as 'members of the family'. No central register of horse numbers exists, although pure-bred animals may be registered with one or other of the forty or so horse and pony breed societies. The majority, however, including those used for competition purposes, are of mixed breed and are therefore unregistered. It has been estimated that there are, in addition, between 12 000 and 13 000 donkeys in the United Kingdom of which 90 per cent could be classed as companion animals.

The purchase value of individual equines varies considerably, although the average price for a riding pony is about £500, and for a horse about £1000. Animals are generally sold privately on a 'word of mouth' basis, through breed societies and riding clubs, or through advertisements in one of the many horse and riding journals. A small number of individuals breed horses and ponies for a living – generally for competition purposes such as show jumping – but it is difficult to obtain an accurate estimate of the total annual value of horse and pony sales for the country as a whole.

4.1.4   Cage birds

The present budgerigar population is estimated at 1.8 million birds in 1.1 million homes. This represents a substantial decline from the 4 million recorded in 1963. There are probably only one tenth as many pet canaries, a small but still substantial number of zebra finches and cockatiels, and even smaller numbers of imported exotic species, such as parrots and mynah birds (see §4.1.7). The majority of common cage birds are home-bred in small aviaries or bird rooms, and sold through local advertisements, pet shops, and garden centres. Prices range from £2 to £3 for a zebra finch, up to £8 for a budgerigar. As with cats very few people earn an adequate living from breeding cage birds. Assuming an average lifespan of around eight years, 250 000 birds a year are needed to maintain the present population. This represents an annual market value of about £1 million.

4.1.5   Small mammals

Population statistics on small mammal pets are sparse. The principal species are rabbits, guinea-pigs, Syrian hamsters, and Mongolian gerbils. Rats, mice, chinchillas, and other small rodents are also kept, although their total commercial value is relatively negligible. The rabbit is the dominant species in this category and it probably outnumbers all the others put together. Excluding those bred for the table, about one million rabbits are kept by 3 to 4 per cent of British households. Common varieties, such as Dutch and New Zealand whites, can be bought in pet shops for as little as £5, while lop-eared and dwarf rabbits fetch twice as much. Thanks to the proverbial fertility of rabbits, many are acquired for nothing. Guinea-pigs, gerbils, and hamsters are each kept by between 1 and 2 per cent of households, and the total population of each is about 250 000. Pet shop prices range from £2 to £5, with some guinea-pigs costing a little more, and many animals change hands for nothing. The total annual market value of small mammals is probably no more than £2 million.

4.1.6   *Aquaria and aquarium fish*

The common goldfish is probably still the most popular species for home aquaria and, together with other cold freshwater species, they represent about 25 per cent of the live fish trade, and an annual market value of around £4 million. In commercial terms, the tropical fish trade is far more substantial. According to 1983 figures, the annual retail value of tropical aquarium species imported into Britain amounted to more than £21 million. (Roughly 85 per cent of these were freshwater species, and 50 to 60 per cent of these were captive bred.) This figure takes no account of the even larger sums spent on aquarium accessories (see §4.2.4). Statistics up to 1983 suggest that the aquarium trade is still expanding in the UK, although British imports represent only about 3 per cent of the world market (Wood 1985).

In all, about one in ten households possess an aquarium and, since most will contain several fish, the total numbers are likely to be considerable. In many cases, the cost of the aquarium and its accessories, will exceed the value of the fish themselves.

4.1.7   *Wild and exotic animals*

The importation and keeping of wild animals as pets is controlled by a variety of measures in the UK. Britain is a party to CITES (the Convention on International Trade in Endangered Species of Wild Fauna and Flora) which requires it to control and report the import or export of any species listed in Appendices, I, II, and III of the Convention. Appendix I (endangered) species may not be imported for primarily commercial purposes. The import of Appendix I, II, and III species is regulated by the Endangered Species (Import and Export) Act 1976, The Wildlife and Countryside Act 1981, and EEC Regulation No. 3626/82 which require the importer to have a valid import permit as well as an export permit from the country of export (unless the latter is another EEC member state). Quarantine restrictions apply to all imported wild birds and mammals, and the Dangerous Wild Animals Act 1976 also restricts and licenses the keeping of large, potentially dangerous, or venomous wild animals by private individuals. Despite these measures, certain groups of exotic species, particularly birds, reptiles, and aquarium fish, are subject to relatively intense commercial trade. Unfortunately, statistics currently available do not permit an accurate estimate of the total value of this trade in financial terms.

A general idea of the extent of the trade in exotic pets can be obtained by looking at certain specific groups. In 1982 and 1983 – the most recent years for which reasonably accurate figures are available – something over 20 000 wild parrots were imported into the UK annually. All of these birds were listed in Appendix II of CITES. The majority came from Indonesia, Tanzania, Senegal, and Guyana, and their retail prices ranged from roughly £35 for the smaller, less colourful species to as much as £3000 for a Palm Cockatoo, *Probisciger aterrimus*. If one assumes an average value of £75 per bird, the annual retail trade in parrots alone may be worth as much as £1.5 million. There is some evidence, however, that trade is declining. The import figures for 1982 and 1983 were less than half those reported for 1980. British imports are also well below those of some other importing countries. Japan, for example, imported over 100 000 parrots in 1981, and the USA imported an average of 225 000 per year during the period 1981–1984 (Broad 1986).

Trade in exotic aquarium fish has already been discussed above (see §4.1.6).

4.2 SERVICING COMPANION ANIMALS

4.2.1 *Pet foods*

The food given to pet animals is generally of three types: (i) specially manufactured food supplying all or part of the animal's nutrient requirements, (ii) fresh, unprocessed food prepared by the owner, and (iii) scraps or titbits from meals consumed by people. Manufactured pet food is by far the largest category. The pet food industry began in 1860 with James Spratts' 'Meat Fibrine Dog Cake'. It grew slowly to an annual retail value of £42.5 million in 1962, but in the last twenty years business has expanded to £810 million a year for cat and dog food, plus another £5 million for packeted bird seed (Pet Food Manufacturers Association figures for 1987). The industry believes that it is currently supplying about 55 and 75 per cent, respectively, of all nutrients eaten by dogs and cats. Fresh foods and scraps presumably make up the difference. Manufactured foods are dominated financially by canned products, although, in terms of nutrients supplied, dry and semi-moist foods provide just over half the total for dogs and cats together.

For raw materials the pet food industry relies heavily on the by-products and surpluses of the human food industry. The required nutrient composition is carefully formulated, often with the addition of quantitatively minor but nevertheless essential vitamins and minerals. Most of the meats are offals obtained from abattoirs licensed for the slaughter of cattle, pigs, and sheep. Poultry and rabbit trimmings and offal are also widely used. Whale meat has not been used by members of the PFMA since 1972. Because of public antipathy and the prohibitive costs of collection, storage, and shipment, kangaroo meat is never used in UK pet foods. Horse meat is only available to the industry in very small quantities as the vast majority is exported for human consumption. Fish is obtained either as trimmings from the processed or frozen fish industry, or as surpluses from glut catches. A small proportion is imported specially; notably sockeye or red salmon and tuna. The principal cereal used in pet food is wheat. Much of this is damaged at harvest or subsequently, and is considered unsuitable for milling into flour for human consumption. Some cereal products are also obtained as by-products from milling speciality flours. The only other cereal used in substantial quantities is maize. According to PFMA figures, the industry utilized 412 000 tonnes of meat and meat by-products, 58 000 tonnes of fish, and 152 000 tonnes of cereals in 1986.

About a hundred companies constitute the pet food industry in the UK, of which about 85 have production plants situated in this country. The PFMA has 70 members (1986) who together represent roughly 90 per cent of the total market. Four of these companies manufacture about 75 per cent of all prepared pet food sold in Britain. The industry employs about 6000 people in all, and large factories are situated in Barrhead, Liverpool, Melton Mowbray, Peterborough, Southall (London), Wisbech, Worksop, and Yatton (Avon).

4.2.2   *Veterinary services*

Professional health care for companion animals has grown steadily over the last thirty or so years, and now it accounts for at least half of the veterinary profession's work. Some large urban practices do no farm animal work at all, while rural practices often include a partner who specializes in small animal work. A 1985 survey (*Veterinary Record*, **118**, 1986) by the British Veterinary Association and the Society of Practising Veterinary Surgeons provides the latest published data on the cost of veterinary care for companion animals. In this survey 1700 practices were identified and approached, of which 373 participated. Of these, 43 per cent were exclusively concerned with small animal practice and employed an average of 2.54 veterinarians; 17 per cent worked with large animals and employed 4.08 veterinarians, while 40 per cent were mixed practices which employed 4.1 veterinarians. Extrapolating these figures nationally, and assuming that 60 per cent of the 'mixed' work involved small animals, gives a total of 5815 veterinary surgeons of whom the equivalent of 3528 were engaged full-time in small animal practice. A further 7000 or so lay staff would also be employed in this area. In terms of income, 61 per cent of fees were derived from small animal work and a further 6 per cent from horses. Median turnover per small animal practitioner was £45 512 *per annum*. Private enquiries, however, suggested that average turnover was somewhat higher – around £50 000 – or a total national turnover of about £176 million. Allowing for inflation since 1985 and the growth of the companion animal population, the figure is now probably closer to £200 million a year. This equates to about £16 per head of the dog and cat population. About 40 per cent of turnover in a small animal practice can be attributed to vaccinations. Neutering, worming, and disinfestations account for about 30 per cent, and the remaining 30 per cent represents more elaborate treatments, including diagnostic tests.

Insurance against the cost of veterinary treatment has become popular in recent years. Routine treatments such as vaccinations are excluded, but for a premium of £16 to £30 a year, the owner is reimbursed for fees and/or the cost of replacing a pet killed accidentally or dying prematurely in some instances. Pet insurance has an annual turnover of between £4 and £5 million, and this figure is expected to double within the next few years. Staff employed number only a hundred or so.

4.2.3   Boarding and quarantine kennels

The business of boarding companion animals, chiefly dogs and cats, has grown considerably in recent years probably as a consequence of the increase in the number of people taking extended holidays. Since the passing of the Animal Boarding Establishments Act 1963, all boarding kennels and catteries must be licensed annually by their local authority and conform to certain statutory requirements, such as providing adequate heating and appropriate facilities. They are also subject to periodic inspection by the authority's representative who may be a veterinary surgeon. No central register is kept so the number of kennels and catteries cannot be assessed accurately. The 'Yellow Pages' telephone directory for the whole country lists well over 4000, although a more realistic figure for those actively operating is probably somewhere between 3500 and 4000. Probably around half of these are run as secondary sources of income, often by married women. Many also function as breeding kennels, and some are attached to veterinary surgeries. Some boarding establishments are open only during the summer months and, occasionally, during the Christmas and Easter holiday seasons. In the more affluent south-east of England, many find sufficient business to remain open all year round. The only full-time employees in most kennels and catteries are the owners. Additional part-time staff tend to be employed during busy periods.

Most boarding kennels have an annual turnover below the VAT limit of £21 300 (1987 figure). Only a few hundred can house more than fifty animals which, with an average of 30 per cent occupancy over the year and a price per animal of between £3 and £5 per day, would yield a gross income of £19 000 per annum. From this figure must be deducted the costs of food, heating, rates, and other overheads. It is therefore clear that profit is not the primary concern of the majority of persons engaging in this exceptionally time-consuming occupation. The total national turnover of boarding kennels and catteries is unlikely to exceed £50 million annually.

In financial terms, the most profitable establishments are those with authorized quarantine facilities. These are less restricted by seasonal fluctuations in business, since animals are being imported all year round, and all mammals (with the exception of horses) must undergo six months quarantine against rabies. About 70 such establishments exist in Britain. Owing to stringent regulations on housing and fencing, their overheads are substantial and it is unlikely that any has an annual financial turnover of less than £10 000. In all, business is probably worth between £1 and £2 million per year.

4.2.4   Pet accessories

In terms of its economic importance, the supply of pet accessories and equipment is second only to the pet-food industry. The business covers an enormously diverse range of relatively essential items, such as toys, treats, patent medicines, grooming equipment, feeding bowls, cages, hutches, kennels, aquaria, and their fittings; as well as such luxuries as toiletries, cosmetics, personalized cat-flaps, and electrically-heated dog beds. A well-stocked pet shop will sell at least 500 separate items, including animals and pet-food (about 5 per cent of manufactured food is sold through such establishments). Many also supplement their income, to a greater or lesser extent, by selling gardening products. Following criticism of their treatment and inadequate socialization of puppies and kittens, pet shop sales of dogs and cats have dropped sharply in recent years. They remain, however, important suppliers of cage-birds, small mammals, fish, and various exotic animals. A recent survey revealed that only 7 per cent sold puppies compared with 13 per cent who purveyed tarantulas (*Pet Product Marketing Magazine*, April, 1987).

Because of the diversity of the pet accessory trade, there are few reliable statistics on financial turnover. A 1983 Euromonitor survey valued the total annual trade at £130 million. Cosmetics and medicines accounted for nearly a third of this figure, and aquaria and aquarium accessories nearly a quarter. A survey by PPM Magazine estimated the average weekly turnover of pet shops at £1452 (£75 000 per annum). Since there are about 2000 pet shops in Britain, this would give a total national turnover of £150 million. This figure includes sales of pet-foods, animals, and gardening items, but excludes pet accessories sold through garden centres or pharmacists. The 711 shops that participated in the PPM survey employed an average of 2.27 full-time and 2.36 part-time staff, giving a national total of about 9000 employees. Many others are, of course, employed in the manufacture and wholesale marketing of pet accessories.

Pet shops are regulated by The Pet Animals Act 1951 which prohibits the selling of animals in streets and public places, and to children under the age of twelve. Licences for the keeping of pet shops are granted by local authorities, subject to evidence that the animals are properly accommodated and cared for, and that adequate arrangements exist to prevent fires or the spread of infectious disease.

4.2.5   Grooming

Grooming is another service available to cats and dogs, primarily the latter. The Pet Trade and Industry Association lists about 400 grooming establishments – commonly known as poodle parlours – amongst its membership. Many are run in conjunction with pet shops or boarding kennels. The work is labour intensive and hence expensive. The gross annual income of a full-time grooming establishment can hardly be less than £20 000, if it is to provide a living wage after deduction of rent, rates, heating, equipment, and other overheads. The total market value must be in the region of £10 million per annum, and those actively employed probably number between 1000 and 2000.

4.3 SUBSIDIARY ACTIVITIES – BREEDING AND SHOWING

As noted earlier in this report (see §2.4), companion animals often serve a variety of different functions. In terms of its extent and economic significance, the breeding and competitive display of companion animals by hobbyists is by far the most important of these subsidiary roles. Although people have been breeding domestic animals selectively for thousands of years, it is only within the last century or so that companion animals have been bred solely for exhibition purposes; that is, to satisfy the 'fancy' of the breeder. Around the middle of the nineteenth century, the hobby of breeding and showing pet animals became a popular and respectable middle-class leisure activity, and this soon led to the first organized dog-show at Newcastle-upon-Tyne in 1859, and the first cat-show at Crystal Palace in 1871. Other pets rapidly followed suit. The Australian budgerigar, first imported in 1840, also attracted its own clique of fanciers, and even the humble house mouse became the subject of a National Mouse Club in 1895. Every popular pet species now has its so-called 'fancy', although those involving dogs, cats, horses, and budgerigars are, predictably, the largest.

4.3.1 *Dogs*

In practice (though not in law) the Kennel Club, founded in 1873, has a complete monopoly over the exhibition of pure-bred dogs in the United Kingdom. It also controls working (obedience) trials and field trials for gundogs. Only one dog-show – namely Crufts – is organized and run by the Club itself. The remaining 7000 or so shows are run by various dog clubs and societies around the country, although each must be licensed or authorized by the Club, if registered dogs are exhibited. Twenty-six of these (including Crufts) are general championship shows at which all registered breeds can be displayed. They have a combined annual income of about £1.5 million, and make a yearly profit of roughly £250 000. Attendance figures vary, but Crufts, the best known, attracts about 85 000 visitors and several thousand exhibitors each year.

In addition to controlling events, the Kennel Club grants registered 'affixes'. These are words, commonly anagrams or place names, which the owner can attach to the names of the dogs that he or she breeds, and which are transferred if the animal acquires a new owner. About 30 000 such affixes are in use at present, which gives a fair indication of the current size of the dog fancy. Interest within the fancy ranges from ownership of one or two show dogs to a full-time occupation involving several breeding bitches, the sale of surplus puppies, and the supply of stud dogs for service at a fee (currently from £50 upwards, depending on the quality of the sire). Pedigree British dogs are highly valued in other countries, and between 5000 and 10 000 puppies and young dogs are exported annually.

Over 600 breed clubs and another 600 general canine societies are registered with the Kennel Club, and somewhere in the region of 20 000 dog-owners and breeders belong to at least one of these organizations. About 100 of these clubs hold field trials for gundogs under Kennel Club regulations. Obedience trials involving working breeds, such as border collies and German shepherd dogs, are even more popular. About 500 training clubs are registered and organize both classes and competitions. The latter include formal obedience tests and the recent sport of agility trials – the canine equivalent of showjumping in horses.

Legislation controlling the breeding of dogs is contained in The Breeding of Dogs Act 1973. Under the Act any premises where more than two bitches are kept for the purpose of breeding for sale must be licensed by the local authority. Evidence of suitable accommodation and care, and adequate provisions for the prevention of fire or the spread of disease is required for a licence to be granted. Unscrupulous dog-breeders and dealers have, nevertheless, found ways of circumventing these regulations (see §6.2.4).

4.3.2   *Cats*

The National Cat Club was founded in 1887 and, apart from the war years, has held a show annually ever since. After several rival clubs had broken away during the early years, cat fanciers realized the need for a controlling authority to regulate matters. The Governing Council of the Cat Fancy (GCCF), formed in 1908, serves essentially the same role as the Kennel Club, though without the latter's social functions or its wealth.

The GCCF has 94 affiliated breed clubs with a combined membership of about 35 000. Most cat fanciers, however, belong to several clubs so the actual number of persons breeding and showing cats is probably somewhere between eight and ten thousand. Ninety-four separate cat-shows are licensed each year by the GCCF. Public attendance in total is approximately 80 000 (about the same as attendance at Crufts). Only two cat-shows, the National and the Supreme, attract more than 1000 exhibitors. The GCCF registers about 30 000 kittens each year. The Cat Association, a rival cat registering authority, was established a few years ago but it does not appear to have made much progress.

4.3.3   *Horses and ponies*

According to a National Equestrian Survey commissioned by the British Horse Society there are more than 3 250 000 regular horse and pony riders in Britain. Of these, about two thirds are adults (over 16) and the remainder are young riders. Riding clubs for adults have a national membership of about 45 000, and the Pony Club has 366 regional and local branches and roughly 35 000 young members. Various kinds of specialist equestrian groups are also affiliated to the BHS, including roughly 5000 dressage members, 6000 horse trial, and 700 long distance competitors. The total membership of the BHS currently stands at over 38 000, an increase of 12 000 since 1978. About 40 different breed societies also cater to the owners of specialist breeds, such as Welsh or Dartmoor Ponies.

Vast numbers of equestrian events, including shows, rallies, and games, are organized by the various horse and pony societies and clubs. A recent issue of the magazine *Horse and Hound*, for example, listed over a hundred separate local and national events for a single week in April 1987. Such events are highly competitive, although participants generally compete for colourful rosettes rather than cash prizes.

Since most riders in Britain do not own their own steeds, the majority hire them from riding schools. About 530 riding schools are approved by the BHS and are inspected twice yearly by representatives of the Society. Another 500 or so function without BHS approval. Under The Riding Establishments Acts 1964 and 1970, all riding schools and establishments which hire out horses for riding must be licensed by their local authority. Licences are issued subject to satisfactory inspection by veterinary practitioners authorized for this purpose by the Royal College of Veterinary Surgeons and the British Veterinary Association. Licences must be renewed annually.

4.3.4   Cage-birds

Although the popularity of cage-birds as household pets has declined over the past 25 years, the fancy seems as strong as ever. The National Exhibition of Cage and Aviary Birds, which has been held annually for the last 50 years, attracts roughly 1000 exhibitors and public attendance approaching 20 000. It is an extremely diversified fancy owing to the number of different bird species involved. About 1200 separate bird clubs exist within the fancy, and by far the largest is the Budgerigar Society, founded in 1925, and with a current membership of around 6000. Another few thousand budgerigar fanciers belong to local Area Societies. At the World Championship Budgerigar Show in 1985, 700 entrants exhibited about 6000 birds.

Before the introduction of the budgerigar in 1840, canaries were the most popular cage-birds in Britain. Although they are now outnumbered by budgerigars ten to one, the fancy continues to thrive. The Yorkshire Canary Club, for example has over 300 members, and its annual show at Shipley exhibits 700 birds. In all, canary fanciers probably number between 1500 and 2000. Other popular avian species, each with its own fancy, include zebra finches, mynah birds, lovebirds, cockatiels, and a variety of other parrots. Racing pigeons, with an estimated population of 10 million birds, outnumber most other pets aside from fish. Although some would regard them as companion animals, they are excluded from this study because, like greyhounds and racehorses, they are kept primarily for competitive purposes (see Chapter 2).

4.3.5   Small mammals

Rabbits and rodents, such as guinea-pigs, rats, mice, hamsters, and gerbils, are also the subjects of various societies and clubs. Rabbit fanciers form the largest group, with perhaps 10 000 active breeders and exhibitors. The remaining species attract something in the region of 3000 fanciers altogether. The largest annual show is the Bradford Championship with roughly 900 exhibitors and a public attendance of about 4000.

4.3.6   *Aquaria and aquarium fish*

The fish fancy is strong, with about 500 separate clubs and societies affiliated to the British Federation of Aquarists. Individual clubs and societies hold their own shows and, in addition, there are four major national events each year: the Aquarium Fish Keeping Exhibition at Sandown Park race course, the British Aquarist Festival at the G-Mex Exhibition Hall in Manchester, the Yorkshire Aquarist Festival at Queen's Hall in Leeds, and the Scottish Aquarist Festival in Motherwell.

4.4   THE COST TO THE OWNER

Market research reveals that roughly half of all households in Britain contain at least one companion animal. Of these, 24 per cent keep dogs, 20 per cent keep cats, 10 per cent possess aquaria, 6 per cent have budgerigars, and various smaller percentages own other cage-birds, small domestic mammals, and a variety of other pets (the total is greater than 50 per cent since many households keep more than one animal). The economic significance of supplying and servicing these animals has already been discussed. The cost to individual pet-owners is now considered.

4.4.1   *Dogs*

The average dog costs its owner roughly £156 per year, of which £115 is spent on food, £16 on veterinary services, £10 on accessories, £8 on boarding and training fees, and £7 on purchase price (averaged across the lifetime of the animal). The first year's costs are substantially higher than average since they include purchase price, larger food bills, and greater outlay on equipment and veterinary services. The figures provided assume a dog of medium size (15 kg), average longevity (ten years), obtained as a puppy, and fed exclusively on medium-priced manufactured dog-food. In reality, only about half the food consumed by Britain's dogs is produced by the pet-food industry, but the average cost of the remainder is unlikely to be significantly more or less since it ranges in quality from scraps to prime fillet steak. The figures given are estimates of average expenditure rather than those recommended by experts. Only about one owner in five, for example, has his or her dog inoculated every year, as recommended by veterinarians.

4.4.2   *Cats*

The average annual cost of cat-ownership works out as £157: £130 for food, £16 for veterinary services, £8 for accessories, £2 for boarding fees, and £1 for purchase price (averaged over the pet's lifetime). The calculation assumes that all cats are about the same size and longevity (six years), that most are cross-bred and therefore cost little or nothing to obtain, that kittens eat the same food as adults, and that cats are fed entirely on one of the more expensive manufactured foods. In fact, about 75 per cent of cats' food is manufactured by the pet-food industry. Nearly all of the remainder are fed on fresh food rather than scraps. As with dogs, the figures represent what is actually spent, not what ought to be, since only about 20 per cent of owners have their animals vaccinated annually, as recommended.

4.4.3 *Horses and ponies*

Horses and ponies are the most expensive companion animals to keep, and also require facilities such as grazing or stabling which are beyond the reach of the majority of urban dwellers. Actual costs to the owner vary depending on whether the animal is grass-fed (and shares grazing with other animals) or stabled, the latter being more expensive. The average grass-fed pony or horse costs its owner around £630 per year, whereas a stabled animal will cost nearly twice as much to keep. These figures include the cost of additional food and nutrients, insurance, tack, veterinary services, and shoeing, but do not include the purchase price which varies from about £500 for a pony to £1000 for the average riding horse. Assuming an equal ratio of grass-fed and stabled animals, and an average equine longevity of 25 years, British horse and pony owners may be spending of the order of £450 million per year on their animals. This figure does not take into account the money spent on hiring horses for riding.

4.4.4 *Cage-birds*

The initial outlay for common species such as budgerigars and canaries includes a modest purchase price (£5 to £8) and perhaps £25 to £35 for a cage and its various accessories. Thereafter, ongoing costs include bird seed, grit, sand or sanded sheets, and the occasional piece of cuttlefish bone, millet, and green-stuffs. Spreading the initial costs over six years (the average lifespan of these birds), the probable annual cost is about £20. This would represent a national outlay of about £40 million a year. Considering their higher purchase price, their sometimes greater longevity, and their more specialized feeding and housing requirements, many exotic species of birds are considerably more expensive to keep.

4.4.5 *Small mammals*

In addition to their purchase price (£2 to £10), rabbits and pet rodents cost about 50 pence a week to feed. Add to this the cost of cages and hutches and, perhaps, one veterinary consultation per lifetime, and the average annual expenditure is probably no more than £35. The total population of these animals is about 2 million, representing a national outlay of around £70 million a year.

4.4.6   *Aquaria and aquarium fish*

The cost of setting up and stocking an aquarium varies from £50 to about £250, depending on size, quality of equipment, and the species of fish involved. A small coldwater aquarium equipped with filter, gravel, plants, ornaments, and a few goldfish is comparatively inexpensive to set up, whereas a large (3 × 2 × 1.5 ft) tropical aquarium with heating, lighting, and other accessories is correspondingly costly. Ongoing maintenance costs also vary considerably depending on electricity consumption for filters, heating, and lighting, and the rate at which plants and fish need to be replaced. One London wholesaler estimates, however, that tropical aquaria cost between £25 and £40 *per annum* to maintain. Although it is impossible to calculate a national figure for the total annual outlay on aquaria and aquarium fish, it is likely to be in the region of £60 million (the total market value of aquarium and fish sales in Britain).

4.5   SUMMARY

Judging from the evidence presented in this chapter, British pet-owners spend nearly £2500 million each year on their animals, or approximately £50 per head of the total population or £150 per household. The total annual cost of dogs and cats works out at about £1880 million; derived from manufactured food sales (£810 million), veterinary care (£188 million), accessories (£150 million), boarding and training (£60 million), purchase (£50 million), and food other than that specially manufactured (about £600 million). To obtain the gross figure, the cost of all companion animals – cage birds, small mammals, aquarium fish and, especially, horses and ponies, must also be added. Such figures, however, do not include additional expenditure on such things as books and magazines about pets, society and club membership fees, or the cost of travel to and from shows, exhibitions, and events involving companion animals. In all, pet-keeping therefore represents one of the most popular leisure activities in this country, and around it has grown a considerable body of industrial, commercial, and recreational interests which provide many thousand of people with full- and part-time employment.

Despite the extent of the phenomenon, our knowledge of people's motives for keeping such animals, or the benefits which accrue from this type of relationship, is surprisingly insubstantial.

5   The benefits of pet-ownership

Domestic animals confer a huge variety of practical benefits on Western society. As well as providing sources of food and raw materials, such as wool and leather, their behaviour is also harnessed and exploited in various beneficial ways. Until comparatively recently, draught animals, such as horses and oxen, provided all the agricultural labour and public transport now generated by machines and fossil fuels. Although their value in this respect is now negligible in the industrial West, horses continue to retain an important role in sport and recreation. Dogs are still used for herding sheep, guarding property, and many other practical tasks, and they have also become the focus of a considerable range of sporting and recreational activities. In addition to all these obvious benefits, many domestic species – the so-called 'companion animals' – furnish their owners with less obvious social and psychological rewards which are difficult to evaluate in economic terms, but which are nevertheless enormously important to the people involved. Perhaps because they are difficult to measure or quantify, the psychosocial benefits of companion animal ownership have received relatively little attention from scientists. Within the last ten or so years, however, a growing body of research has begun to shed light on the nature of this relationship with companion animals, and its potential value in human terms.

5.1   COMPANION ANIMALS AND CHILDREN

Because it tends to be taken for granted, people seldom notice the extent to which the worlds of children are dominated by animals. Animal toys, such as rabbits or teddy bears, are often the first gifts babies receive. Today these are usually either knitted or made from artificial fur, but a generation ago animal fur was commonly used. Real animals play little part in the early months of an infant's life. Household pets are usually kept away from babies, and cots and prams are sometimes netted to prevent cats intruding. It is widely held that cats can suffocate babies by lying on them, although there seems to be little if any evidence supporting this belief. Cats and dogs are usually first encountered when the child is placed to kick on the floor and, later, begins to crawl. At this stage, most children show intense interest in pets and will try to move towards them or grasp their fur. Parents often call children's attention to companion animals and name them and, perhaps because of this, names of pets – cat, dog, or their childish equivalents – are often among the first words used by children, not infrequently preceding the use of 'mama' and 'dada'. Even as early as two years of age, some children will direct social behaviour toward family pets, and will also respond sympathetically to real or imagined feelings in companion animals (Zahn-Waxler *et al.* 1985).

The first books that children are given to look at are almost exclusively about animals; chiefly cats, dogs, and farm animals. Real animals, as well as innumerable animal puppets and cartoons, also feature prominently in children's television programmes. *Blue Peter*, for example, regularly features live dogs and cats in the studio, and many items concern such subjects as pet care, unusual pets, animal sanctuaries, and wild animals. Real or imaginary animal characters are also frequently the subjects of story books for older children – the tales of Beatrix Potter, *Babar the Elephant*, *Little Grey Rabbit*, *Winnie the Pooh*, *Sam Pig*, *The Wild Things*, *Rupert Bear* and *Doctor Dolittle*, to name just a few of the most famous.

No entirely satisfactory explanation exists for this prominence of animals in children's literature and television. Indeed, the topic appears to have been largely ignored by child psychologists, and none of the major textbooks on the subject makes any reference to the role of companion animals or animals in general in the child's world. It has been suggested that stories involving animal characters, because they are less realistic, allow the exploration of potentially dangerous or upsetting themes. Certainly such themes are obvious in many of these stories – the simple morality of *Tom Kitten*, the evocation of the terrors of the night in *The Wild Things*, the patriarchal family in *Bambi*, and the class structure of *Babar* – but this hardly seems sufficient explanation since such themes are explored in all sorts of writing for children, whether or not animals are involved. Whatever the reason, it is clear that many children find it easy to identify with animals and animal characterizations. Animals in stories do things which are impossible in the real world and, for the child, they perhaps represent a sort of symbolic entrance into a world of fantasy and make-believe where reality is temporarily suspended and the imagination is given full rein. Animals occupy a similar role in the folklore and mythology of a great many cultures. In our own, it appears, this use of animals is most clearly expressed and exploited during childhood.

Surveys in Britain and the United States have revealed that companion animals are more common in households with children (Franti *et al.* 1980; Messent and Horsfield 1985). Such statistics presumably reflect the popular belief among parents that children benefit from the company of pets. The nature and extent of the putative benefits remain, however, largely unstudied. Psychiatrists and psychotherapists working with children have suggested a variety of important functions for childhood pets. Many young children, for example, derive comfort and reassurance from contact with soft objects – blankets, bits of fur, and stuffed animal toys. Family pets are also frequently used in this way. So-called 'transitional objects' of this kind are thought to help children towards the development of independence by providing them with mobile or portable sources of comfort and security during their explorations of the world (Winnicott 1953). Animals, of course, have the advantage over inanimate objects in that they can initiate interactions, return affection, and participate directly in the child's activities.

Pets also play an important role in the elaborate fantasy games of children, which, for various reasons, they often find difficult to play with their peers. Through the medium of fantasy play with companion animals, and through general discussions about their behaviour, children also seem to be able to express, and so come to terms with, subconscious doubts, worries, and fears. For instance, childrens' earliest experiences of central life events, such as birth, death, and sexuality, often come from owning or watching companion animals. Such episodes provide a useful opportunity to learn about and discuss topics which tend, otherwise, to be suppressed or avoided. Child psychiatrists occasionally exploit this phenomenon by introducing pets (either their own or the child's) into their therapeutic sessions. In such situations, animals seem to act as 'ice-breakers'; softening the child's initial hostility and reserve, and providing a comparatively neutral focus for the discussion of potentially emotive subjects (Levinson 1969; Sherick 1981).

Among older children, animals often become important social companions. Children talk to and confide in their pets, incorporate them into physical games and sports, and take them for company on solitary walks and expeditions. Sometimes a child will regard a dog or a riding pony as his or her 'best friend' and the relationship with the animal may become a welcome escape from difficult relationships within the home or at school. The special kind of uncritical, non-judgemental affection provided by companion animals is probably particularly important in this respect. As the frequent objects of hobbies and recreational activities, animals can also promote contacts and friendships between children with similar interests. They may also have a more direct effect on the development of children's social skills. A recent study, for example, found that pet-owning adolescents were both more popular and more sensitive at decoding non-verbal facial expressions than non-pet-owning children of the same age. (Guttmann *et al.* 1985).

Finally, it is widely believed that pet-ownership serves a valuable educative function for children. The business of looking after, feeding, cleaning, training, and caring for companion animals is thought to teach children all sorts of desirable adult traits, such as gentleness, personal responsibility, dependability, and self-control (Levinson 1972; Salmon and Salmon 1983). It undoubtedly provides an opportunity to express nurturant behaviour and, like playing with dolls, may help to introduce children at an early age to many of the experiences and responsibilities of parenthood. As already stated, companion animals also provide instructive lessons on many basic facts of life. In addition, close contact with pets during childhood is thought to inculcate a deeper understanding and empathy for animals in general. Tentative evidence supporting this idea has come from recent research on 8 to 10 year olds (Bowd 1984). Pet-owning children in this study expressed more positive feelings about animals and exhibited fewer fears of them than a corresponding sample of non-pet-owners. Long-term, adult attitudes to companion animals, such as dogs and cats, certainly appear to be influenced by childhood experiences. People brought up with dogs, for example, tend to remain dog-lovers throughout their lives. Those brought up with cats prefer cats, and those raised with both tend to remain affectionately disposed toward both species (Serpell 1981).

5.2   COMPANION ANIMALS AND ADULTS

Recent interest in the benefits of pet-ownership for adults has been stimulated by a series of studies carried out at the Universities of Maryland and Pennsylvania within the last ten years. The first of these studies examined the effects of social relationships and personality on the survival of 92 heart-attack sufferers. Each of the subjects in this study was interviewed in hospital following episodes of either angina pectoris or myocardial infarction. They were tested for mood (since depression is known to be associated with increased risks of heart disease), and they were also asked a battery of questions concerning their social life. Among these were some questions on pet-ownership. Subjects were then followed up a year after being discharged from hospital, at which time 14 of the original 92 had died. As expected, certain types of social contact (or a lack of them) emerged as important predictors of one-year survival. Contrary to expectation, however, it was found that the pet-owners in the sample had a significantly better chance of surviving than the non-pet-owners (Friedmann *et al.* 1980).

This apparent effect of pet-ownership was not due to the extra physical exercise of walking dogs, since other kinds of pet-owner also seemed to benefit. Nor could it be attributed to pre-existing differences in personality between owners and non-owners (Friedmann *et al.* 1984). Subsequent research suggested that companion animals had a direct effect on the physical states of their owners by calming them in potentially stressful situations. It was found, for example, that people experience reduced heart-rate and blood pressure when stroking or interacting with their pets, even under the somewhat unnerving circumstances of a laboratory experiment (Katcher 1981). Even the mere presence of a companion animal in the same room, whether or not it belonged to the subject and regardless of whether it was handled, could also exert a calming influence on people in similar situations (Friedmann *et al.* 1983). Animals can also serve as relaxing sources of contemplation. In another series of experiments, subjects were asked to sit quietly in front of an aquarium and observe the activities of tropical fish. Again they exhibited marked reductions in blood pressure and, more to the point, the effects were strongest in subjects suffering from high blood pressure (Katcher *et al.* 1984).

Companion animals also seem to enhance the social mobility and acceptability of their owners. Many owners of companion animals, particularly dogs, claim that their pets have helped to increase their circle of acquaintances and have made them new friends. Politicians and other public figures seem to be familiar with this phenomenon, and exploit it by appearing regularly in the press or the media accompanied by their pets. Such effects have been confirmed by research. One psychologist has shown, for example, that pictures or drawings of groups of people are perceived by others in a more positive and less threatening light if an animal, such as a dog or a cat, is included in the scene (Lockwood 1983). Other studies have demonstrated that elderly people with pets receive more spontaneous visits from others (Mugford and M'Comisky 1975), and that people walking their dogs are, on average, involved in more positive social encounters and a greater number of extended conversations than people walking either alone or with small children or babies (Messent 1983). In other words, companion animals appear to act as 'social catalysts' both by making their owners seem more attractive and less threatening, and by initiating interactions with strangers which might not otherwise occur. The physical component of such interactions is probably important. In many Western societies, intense and intimate physical greetings are virtually taboo except between very close friends and relatives. Yet, one can stroke, pet, or fondle a stranger's dog without necessarily violating these unwritten rules of social etiquette. Very recently, it has also been found that the presence of a familiar dog can also promote the resolution of marital conflicts. During counselling, unhappily married couples displayed fewer negative emotions and calmer, less variable, physiological responses when accompanied by their dogs (Levenson and Meek, unpublished data). Precisely how the animal achieves this effect is unknown, although its ability to act as a social catalyst or mediator may again be responsible.

Perhaps the commonest function attributed to companion animals is their ability to serve as antidotes to loneliness and social isolation, both of which are thought to be on the increase in certain sectors of the population. For obvious reasons, the value of pets for the elderly has received particular attention, and a great deal has been written on the subject in recent years (Bustad 1980; Bustad and Hines 1983). It has been argued, for instance, that companion animals not only provide substitutes for lost or diminishing human relationships but also, by requiring care, contribute a sense of routine, purpose, and fulfilment to the lives of elderly and lonely people. This intuitively appealing concept has been somewhat difficult to demonstrate in practice, at least among the elderly (see for example, Lago *et al.* 1985). Although the results of research suggest that pet-ownership can improve the health and morale of some elderly people, particularly those who are highly involved with or attached to their pets, there are also various exceptions. Persons on low income or with failing health, for example, may find the responsibility of caring for an animal more of a burden than a pleasure. It would also be a mistake to assume that all lonely people would necessarily consider a pet a satisfactory substitute for human relationships. Individual attitudes to pets and each person's ability to relate to such animals as social companions undoubtedly affect their value in this respect. When such attitudes are favourable, however, it appears that companion animals can reduce or alleviate some effects of social loss or deprivation. In a study of recently bereaved women, for example, those with strong attachments for their pets reported less grief and less deterioration of health following the death of a spouse than those without pets (Bolin, unpublished data).

In addition to the less tangible social and emotional benefits of pet-ownership, many companion animals also serve a considerable variety of practical and recreational roles. As already described (see §4.3), the keeping, breeding, training, and showing of pets provides an absorbing hobby for thousands of people, and for many it is a lifelong amateur activity which occupies virtually all of their spare time. As an integral part of many field sports, dogs, ponies, and horses also contribute substantially to their owner's overall happiness and physical health. Even the regular daily activity of walking a dog is a valuable source of recreation and exercise for many owners (Serpell 1983). The companionship of dogs can also be an important source of safety and security. The results of a recent study by criminologists, for example, confirmed that the presence of a barking dog in a house acts as a powerful deterrent to burglars and intruders (Bennett and Wright 1984). Significantly, the marked increase in the popularity of large guard dog breeds, such as Dobermanns, Rottweilers and German Shepherds, within the last decade (Edney 1984) has been associated with an apparent rise in national crime rates.

The various ways in which companion animals benefit their owners are clearly complex, and it is difficult to generalize about the underlying mechanisms responsible for their effects. At one level, it appears that companion animals are highly diverting. Interacting with pets or merely watching them seems to divert people's attention away from themselves, and this state of absorption may be associated with a rewarding sense of calmness and relaxation. With certain obvious exceptions, it is also apparent that many people perceive companion animals as essentially friendly, non-threatening creatures, and this positive, reassuring influence is often extended to include both the owner and the situation the animal is in. These phenomena not only help to make people feel calmer and less stressed, but can also contribute indirectly to the owner's social life by making him or her more appealing or attractive to others. The tendency of some companion animals to approach strangers in a friendly and uninhibited way probably enhances social contact by acting, so to speak, as a letter of introduction. This effect of pets is presumably culture-specific, since many societies would not necessarily view dogs, cats, or other pets in such a positive light. It should also be emphasized that, while a pet may promote relaxation or inspire friendship in others, few pet-owners obtain companion animals for these reasons alone..

In surveys, the vast majority of pet-owners stress companionship or friendship as the primary reason for owning a pet and, while these are somewhat nebulous concepts, they probably provide the essential key to understanding the popularity of these animals. Humans possess social as well as material needs, and an increasing amount of medical evidence suggests that positive social relationships and friendships play an important role in maintaining people's mental and physical health. The protective and restorative effects of companionship derive not only from the practical or material assistance we obtain from others, but also from a much less clearly defined sense of being valued or needed. By behaving towards their owners in a highly dependent, possessive, and attentive manner, companion animals are particularly good at inspiring this sense of being needed and loved (Serpell 1986). The resemblance between pets and young children, in this respect, is difficult to ignore. Like children, companion animals need to be cared for and nurtured in order to survive; they enjoy being caressed, cuddled, and played with, and they are relatively uninhibited and uncritical in their overtures of friendship and affection. This is not to suggest that pets (for adults) are merely 'child substitutes', but rather indicates that both pet-ownership and parenthood can offer comparable emotional rewards and an analogous sense of personal fulfilment. Far more research is needed on the social and emotional benefits of pet-ownership, but existing information suggests that the potential value of this relationship has, in the past, been seriously underestimated.

5.3   COMPANION ANIMALS IN THERAPY

The terms 'pet therapy' and 'pet-facilitated therapy' are now widely employed to describe the increasing use of companion animals in various clinical, therapeutic, and remedial contexts. It is difficult to estimate the extent of pet therapy schemes in Britain, since most are conducted on a largely informal basis. In parts of the United States, however, a recent regional survey revealed that roughly 50 per cent of nursing homes and other health facilities were using animals in some form of therapeutic capacity (Olsen *et al.* 1983). Although unconventional from a purely medical standpoint, this use of companion animals is based on relatively simple and straightforward theoretical concepts.

Probably the earliest documented use of animals as therapy occurred at the York Retreat, a famous mental asylum established in the north of England during the late eighteenth century. The Retreat was the creation of William Tuke, a progressive Quaker, who advocated exceptionally liberal and permissive treatment methods. Punishment and restraint were eschewed in favour of a system of rewards for good behaviour, and inmates were allowed to wear their own clothes, engage in simple occupational tasks, and encouraged to help in the care of small domestic animals, such as chickens and rabbits, which inhabited the Retreat's courtyards and gardens. Tuke believed that contact with pet animals helped the insane to develop self-control by 'having dependent upon them creatures weaker than themselves'. A somewhat similar policy was also adopted in 1867 at a residential treatment centre for epileptics at Bethel-Bielefeldt in southern Germany. Bethel has since expanded considerably and now houses over 5000 mentally and physically handicapped patients. Animals – pets, riding horses, working farms, and even a safari park – remain an important part of the treatment milieu.

The current revival of interest in the potential therapeutic value of companion animals derives largely from the work of the American child psychologist, Boris Levinson. During sessions with withdrawn and emotionally disturbed children, Levinson observed that many of his patients responded enthusiastically to his pet dog, Jingles, while they were typically hostile or uncommunicative towards himself. By insinuating himself carefully into this relationship between child and dog, he found he was able to initiate a therapeutic rapport with the child much more quickly than was normally possible. In Levinson's view, the chief therapeutic value of companion animals was their ability to act as social catalysts: first, by stimulating or initiating friendly, playful, and non-threatening social contact; and second, by providing a relatively neutral or 'safe' channel for the discussion of subconscious worries and fears (Levinson 1969). The role of animals was unique, he believed, because, unlike human therapists, they were able to offer unconditional affection without ever being judgemental or critical. Other psychiatrists and psychoanalysts have arrived at similar conclusions. Woods (1965), for example, wrote that because 'the human–pet relationship is one step removed from the highly charged conflictual relationships with persons, many patients are thereby able to see themselves and others with greater clarity, with less denial and repression, and with greater insight.' A questionnaire survey of psychotherapists belonging to the American Psychological Association also found that 21 per cent reported some therapeutic use of animals, and the most common method of use was 'as a vehicle for cultivating or modelling positive interpersonal relationships' (Rice, Brown, and Caldwell 1973).

Levinson gradually expanded his ideas in a series of books and articles, and produced a set of recommendations on the potential therapeutic uses of companion animals. He argued that pet-therapy would be likely to be most effective with withdrawn, uncommunicative, inhibited, autistic, and obsessive–compulsive patients, and in hospitals or institutional settings where people are necessarily separated from the support of relatives and friends. To a large extent his theories have been supported by the results of subsequent research.

5.3.1   *Pets in hospitals and nursing homes*

Psychiatrists at the State University of Ohio were among the first to test Levinson's ideas in a hospital setting. They selected 50 withdrawn and uncommunicative patients at the psychiatric unit where they worked and managed to persuade 47 of them to choose dogs from kennels adjacent to the hospital. Patients were then allowed to interact with their chosen animal at appointed times each day. By the end of the study, 'some improvement' was noted in all patients, and five of them had improved markedly. Contrary to some expectations, patients did not become so attached to their pets that they lost the will to interact with people. Instead, as Levinson predicted, the animal acted as a social catalyst, forging positive links with other patients and staff, and creating 'a widening circle of warmth and approval'. The dogs achieved this, it was argued, by providing patients with a special kind of non-threatening, non-judgemental affection which 'helped to break the vicious cycle of loneliness, helplessness, and social withdrawal' (Corson and O'Leary Corson 1980). These same researchers later went on to examine the effects of pet-facilitated therapy (PFT) in a nursing home for elderly people and, again, reported remarkable successes with some individual patients. One elderly man, for example, spoke a coherent sentence for the first time in 26 years.

In scientific terms these studies were not entirely convincing as the authors made no attempt to eliminate other, more conventional, forms of treatment while their patients were exposed to PFT. They also relied entirely on individual case histories, and there was no matching control group to serve as a valid comparison. Some of these problems have been overcome by more recent research. At a nursing home for elderly people in Melbourne, for example, a study population was divided into separate wards, some of whom received regular contact with the hospital's resident dog, while the others did not. Using a standard series of questionnaires, both groups were then assessed by staff at intervals over a six month period. By the end of the study, patients on the experimental wards were rated as being happier, more alert, more responsive to others, as enjoying life more, having a greater will to live, and having improved relationships with other patients and with staff. All of these changes were statistically significant but, because they were based on the assessments of staff members, they need to be interpreted with caution. The staff involved expected benefits, and it is possible that they unconsciously biased their assessments in the expected direction (Salmon and Salmon 1982). These problems of interpretation are highlighted by a recent attempt to replicate and extend the Melbourne findings. The design of the study was essentially similar – although it lacked a control group – and included behavioural observations of patients and staff before, and at intervals after, the introduction of a therapeutic dog. As in Melbourne, both patients and staff felt that the dog had had a beneficial effect overall, although the staff were more favourable than the patients. The behavioural results, however, suggested that these effects were short-lived. After an initial increase in activity and social interaction a short time after the dog's arrival, most patients gradually reverted to the more solitary behaviour they had shown before the study. Staff morale underwent a more dramatic and longlasting improvement, and certain individual patients – particularly those who had been withdrawn beforehand – seemed to benefit markedly (Winkler *et al.* unpublished data).

Taken together, the results of hospital-based schemes suggest that pet therapy can stimulate transient improvements in social interaction and communication between both patients and staff in a variety of institutional settings. For some individuals, particularly those who are exceptionally withdrawn or isolated from human contact, the technique may initiate longer-term improvements by reconnecting them with the outside world, and rendering them more accessible to conventional forms of psychotherapy. The apparent positive impact of pet therapy on staff morale is also intriguing, and would repay more detailed study. Caring for the elderly, the seriously handicapped, or the terminally ill can place an enormous strain on the emotional resources of medical and nursing staff. As a result, staff turnover is typically high in institutions that cater for these sorts of problems. It is possible that the presence of companion animals can improve the well-being of staff, and lower the rate of attrition, by simply making the hospital environment happier, more enjoyable, and less forbidding.

5.3.2   Pet visiting schemes

When circumstances (or prejudices) do not permit the keeping of resident hospital pets, pet visiting schemes have proved popular. Such schemes are run on a largely voluntary basis by local individuals and groups, and they cater mainly to hospices and the institutionalized elderly. Although they obviously limit the amount of animal contact possible, pet visiting schemes have several advantages. The animal can be kept away from those who dislike or are allergic to pets; neither residents nor staff need feel responsible for the animal's care, and the schemes help to promote contact with members of the surrounding community. In Britain, by far the largest visiting scheme, known as Pro-Dogs Active Therapy (PAT), is organized by the charity Pro-Dogs. More than 2500 members now participate in the PAT Dogs scheme, and over 200 hospitals, hospices, and other institutions are visited on a regular basis (this figure does not include nursing homes, several hundred of which are also visited). Dogs are tested for temperamental suitability before being registered for the scheme, and wear a registration disc on the collar. Their owners are also covered by the necessary insurance.

Although there is no scientific evidence that visiting pets have any positive effect on the health of those they visit, they undoubtedly provide a source of diversion and entertainment, and a welcome break from the dreary routines of hospital and nursing home existence. In their role as social catalysts, pets can also stimulate conversation and interaction and, for some residents, their regular visits may become the high point of the week. The results of one study suggest that pet visiting schemes can also improve the life-satisfaction, mental function, and well-being of elderly nursing home residents (Francis, unpublished data).

5.3.3   Pets in prisons

Perhaps prompted by the famous account of the so-called 'bird man of Alcatraz', prison-based pet therapy schemes have recently become popular, especially in the United States. Although they represent a relatively specialized therapeutic use of companion animals, the rationale behind them is essentially the same as that governing most other pet therapy programmes. The prison inmate, like other institutionalized persons, is isolated from family and friends, deprived of normal social interactions, denied responsibilities, and subjected to a dull and regimented daily routine. More to the point, many adult offenders are obliged to live with these kinds of restrictions for years or even decades. According to theory, not only can the companionship of pets help to make the rigours of prison life more bearable for such people, but may also assist in their rehabilitation. Mutual involvement in the care of animals seems to promote cooperation and tolerance between prison inmates and staff and, in some instances, may lead to the development of small-scale commercial enterprises or community service programmes.

Many animal-based schemes have been established in American penal institutions. Probably the longest running programme began in 1974 at the Oakwood Forensic Center (formerly Lima State Hospital) in Lima, Ohio. Although not strictly-speaking a prison, the Center functions as a maximum-security mental hospital and houses dangerous and violent criminal offenders. Pets, chiefly birds, small mammals, and aquarium fish, were introduced at Oakwood as part of a formal and carefully-monitored programme. According to the organizers, the results have been remarkable. A comparison of wards with and without pets revealed that the incidence of violence and attempted suicide was twice as high on the ward without pets, as was the need for tranquillizing medication (Lee 1983). Unfortunately, the data to substantiate these findings have not been published. A similar scheme also operates at Lorton Correctional Facility, a medium-security prison near Washington DC, where the organizers also report improved morale and cooperation, particularly among the more depressed and withdrawn inmates (Hines 1983).

Other prison-based schemes have placed the emphasis on occupational or vocational programmes involving animals. Purdy Treatment Center for Women in Washington State has instituted a programme of training dogs to assist physically handicapped people. The scheme represents a unique example of cooperation and coexistence between the community and the prison population. Many of the dogs are strays provided by the local Humane Society, and prison inmates are instructed how to train and care for them. Each trainer then works in collaboration with a handicapped individual in order to fit the animal's skills to the precise needs of its future owner. Everyone seems to benefit. Abandoned dogs are found new homes, disabled people acquire useful and affectionate companions, and prisoners develop a valuable and immensely rewarding vocational skill (Hines 1983).

Very few organized animal therapy schemes exist in British prisons. Where they do exist, they are mostly regarded as a means of employment rather than therapy. Several open prisons operate commercial farms of one sort or another, and at Edinburgh Prison cooperative ventures are being developed in collaboration with Edinburgh Zoo and with Stirling University Institute of Aquaculture. In both cases, prisoners are involved with the breeding and husbandry of small animals, such as fish and reptiles, either to contribute to ongoing research

36 Companion Animals in Society

projects, or to help with the conservation of particular endangered species. There would appear to be considerable scope for the expansion of animal-based remedial schemes in UK prisons (Whyte 1987). HM Prison Service regulations, however, do not encourage this sort of innovation, since pets are largely prohibited in most prisons. As a privilege and at the governor's discretion, individual prisoners may be allowed to keep cage birds but not, as a rule, in their own cells.

5.3.4 Companion animals and the physically handicapped

The use of trained animals to assist the handicapped has been established for longer than most forms of animal therapy. The Guide Dogs for the Blind Association, for instance, has been operating for roughly 55 years, and currently has 3750 fully-trained dogs in service. Within the last five years, the principle has also been extended to include the deaf, and dogs are now being trained by Hearing Dogs for the Deaf to assist profoundly deaf people by responding to common household sounds, such as doorbells, telephones, fire alarms, alarm clocks, etc. In the United States and parts of Europe, various organizations also breed and train so-called 'Assistance Dogs' for the physically disabled, although training is often more complex and expensive than it is for guide or hearing dogs. Whereas most blind or deaf people are faced with the same difficulties, each disabled person tends to have unique problems and unique assistance requirements. Similar schemes are currently being developed in Britain. In addition to the performance of physical tasks, assistance dogs can be trained to react to subtle changes in their owner's condition. One dog trained at the Purdy Correction Center is able to warn its owner when she is about to have a life-threatening *grand mal* seizure. The dog immediately nudges her until she stops whatever she is doing, lies down, and rests.

Although the primary purpose of all guide or assistance dogs is to enhance the physical capabilities of their owners, they also provide a host of other social and emotional rewards. Whether blind, deaf, or otherwise physically impaired, many handicapped people feel isolated by their disabilities, and the constant companionship of a dog can do a great deal to relieve their inevitable feelings of loneliness. By reducing their dependence on the help of other people, assistance animals can also improve social confidence and self-esteem. As in other contexts, assistance dogs can act as social catalysts by promoting interactions with other people. This role is particularly important for the handicapped since they carry the social stigma of being different or atypical, and others may feel too embarrassed or awkward in their presence to initiate interactions. Various studies have confirmed that handicapped people are far more likely to be involved in spontaneous conversations or interactions with strangers when they are accompanied by their dogs (Delafield 1976; Zee 1983).

Therapeutic horse-riding or 'hippotherapy' has also been shown to have beneficial effects on disabled and handicapped people, particularly children. Through physical exercise it can improve balance, posture, strength, coordination, flexibility, and range of motion. And, because it is a so-called 'risk exercise' involving the control or mastery of a large and powerful animal, riding also fosters self-confidence, courage, and motivation. Other probable benefits include increased attention span and powers of concentration, and improved emotional control, social awareness, peer relations, and self concept. Although riding for the disabled is most commonly recommended for those with obvious physical handicaps, it can also produce remedial effects in unexpected areas. Children with language disorders, for example, have displayed significant improvements in verbal skills following a course of riding therapy (DePauw 1984; Dismuke 1984).

5.4 SUMMARY

Relationships with companion animals provide people with many benefits, the characteristics of which tend to vary according to a person's age, sex, and circumstances, and the type of pet owned. Like meditation, watching or interacting with animals can induce a state of calmness and relaxation in which bodily processes seem to occur more smoothly. Pet-ownership also appears to promote a higher rate of positive social interaction with others. Companion animals are evidently socially attractive in themselves, and they are often willing and able to initiate spontaneous interactions with strangers without incurring apprehension or hostility on either side. By making people feel safer and more protected, some companion animals, particularly dogs, may also help their owners to cope with isolation and unfamiliar or potentially threatening social situations.

Above all, a pet provides an outlet for nurturant and care-giving behaviour. Through its various gestures of attachment, affiliation, and dependence, it provides its owner with a powerful sense of being valued and needed. Pets can therefore augment their owner's social relationships and, if necessary, provide alternative sources of emotional support when other relationships fail.

Finally, companion animals serve symbolic functions. Perhaps because they occupy a somewhat ambiguous position between humans and animals, pets often become the outlet or the focus for displaced worries, fears, and fantasies about human relationships. As an anthropologist once put it 'animals are good to think', especially when the subject matter is one that arouses serious anxiety or conflict. Through non-threatening relationships with companion animals, people may be able to express and overcome such problems and, hence, restore contact between themselves and others. This is one of the most interesting and least understood roles of companion animals, and it is one that would repay more detailed investigation.

The scope for research in these areas is vast, and the results of clinical and experimental trials have often been inconclusive. However, given the many apparent psychological and emotional rewards of pet-ownership, it is likely that companion animals have an important potential role to play in therapy. Pets should not be regarded as some sort of universal panacea. Nor should they be viewed as a cheap and simple antidote to major social problems such as loneliness or old age. Nevertheless, within limits, they can improve the quality of life for many institutionalized, disturbed, elderly, and handicapped people and, in some cases, interactions with animals may initiate long-term improvements in psychological and physical condition.

6 The problems of pet-ownership

Although lacking many of the more complex ingredients of human interpersonal relationships, relationships with companion animals undoubtedly share many features in common with them. The human tendency to empathize with animals as subjects, and to view them as quasi-persons, allows us to relate to pets and interpret their behaviour as if we were dealing with human friends or relatives. The sense of identification and mutual attachment that arises from this process is the origin of many of the benefits of pet-ownership. But it is also, either directly or indirectly, the source of a variety of problems. Pet-owners, for instance, may become too dependent on their animals, misinterpret or over-interpret their behaviour, or simply expect too much of them. Alternatively, the animal may become a source of difficulties by behaving, for various reasons, in an abnormal or inappropriate fashion, despite the owner's best intentions. More often than not, problems arise through an interaction between these two forces. By virtue of their honorary 'human' status, companion animals enjoy greater legal and moral protection than other kinds of domestic animal. Nevertheless, the fact they *are* animals and not persons, allows people to exploit, mistreat, and abuse them in ways which would be entirely unacceptable within the context of human relationships. As a result, the welfare of these animals is sometimes threatened, and a variety of problems are created for the community in which they live.

6.1 PROBLEMS IN THE OWNER–PET RELATIONSHIP

Despite the ability of humans to communicate their differences through the medium of language, relationships between people are fraught with difficulties, and even the best partnerships are rarely trouble free. It is not altogether surprising, therefore, that problems occur in animal–human relationships where this level of communication is impossible.

6.1.1 *Owner-related problems*

The most common source of problems in the relationship between humans and companion animals is the tendency of people to obtain pets when they lack the time, the resources, the knowledge, or the inclination to provide these animals with adequate care. Caring for a pet, particularly the larger species such as dogs and ponies, is a major responsibility, and failure to recognize this can jeopardize the welfare of the animal and/or create serious difficulties both for the owner and, indirectly, for society. Recurring examples of this type of problem include the abandonment of pets when their owners go on holiday, or the common habit of giving puppies, kittens, and other pets to children as Christmas gifts. A young child may regard such animals as toys and inflict considerable suffering through teasing and mishandling. Even when active cruelty is not involved, few children are willing or able to devote the necessary amount of time to rearing and training such pets and, unless parents are prepared to shoulder much of the responsibility, the animal soon becomes a nuisance. As a result, animal welfare charities are faced with the problem of thousands of abandoned animals each year, many of which must be destroyed (see §6.2.1). Those which are not abandoned, or destroyed are often turned out of the home to roam free during the daytime while the members of the household are at school or at work. So-called 'latch-key' dogs may be a hazard to traffic, other animals, and pedestrians, and are often responsible for fouling footpaths and other public areas (see §6.4). Financial pressures can also put the relationship and the welfare of companion animals at risk. In a recent pilot study, for instance, it was found that incidences of companion animal abuse, neglect and, presumably, abandonment occurred more frequently in families with low incomes (Hutton 1983). Significantly, a substantial proportion of these families also had a history of child abuse or neglect. Family problems – the birth of a new baby, divorce, separation, or bereavement – can also turn beloved companion animals into serious liabilities.

Although their intentions may be laudable, pet-owners sometimes contribute to the development of behaviour problems and physical illness in their pets. Over-indulged companion animals, especially dogs, may become unruly and disobedient, or obese through over-feeding. The owner may also condition the animal inadvertently to engage in undesirable behaviour by either unconsciously rewarding it with attention, punishing it inappropriately, or simply misinterpreting its behaviour. The owner's personality and attitudes are also important. It has been found, for example, that owners with non-authoritarian attitudes are more likely to provoke displays of aggressive dominance from their dogs, while the pets of neurotic owners tend to be more excitable (O'Farrell 1986). Conversely, a minority of owners may project their own fantasies or feelings of inadequacy on to the animal and, as a result, subject it to unnecessary mental and physical suffering or abuse.

Further problems can arise when owners become too socially or emotionally dependent on their pets. Although generally infrequent, sexual relationships between humans and companion animals occur from time to time, and the psychiatric literature reports several cases in which people, for various reasons, have withdrawn from normal social contact and become utterly involved with and dependent on their pets. In such situations, the animal may provide an adequate substitute for human relationships, and the person may feel little inclination to emerge into the real world. In such cases, the eventual death of the animal can provoke a serious emotional crisis, and there have been many examples of people becoming clinically depressed or attempting suicide following the death of a pet. Relationships of this intensity between people and their pets are rare and generally develop from pre-existing psychological problems or social isolation. Nevertheless, many owners become strongly attached to their companion animals and feel a profound sense of loss or bereavement when they die. Unfortunately, the expression of grief over the death or loss of an animal is often considered socially unacceptable, despite the fact that this is a normal and, within reason, healthy reaction (Serpell 1986). Society's unwillingness to take such attachments seriously can itself inflict unnecessary suffering on owners. Some local authorities and officials, for example, specifically ban pets, particularly dogs, from sheltered housing. Prospective pet-owning tenants, most of whom will be elderly, may then be faced with the choice of denying themselves such accommodation or getting rid of one of the few objects of their affection (JACOPIS 1981).

6.1.2 Animal-related problems

Although dogs and cats have associated with people for several thousand years, they still exhibit most of the behaviour patterns of their wild ancestors. Occasionally, these patterns of behaviour may cause serious problems or inconvenience for the owner. Evidence suggests that the majority of dogs display at least some form of undesirable behaviour, and as many as 20 to 25 per cent may engage in activities which constitute a severe nuisance. Cats, on the whole, appear to exhibit fewer such problems, although the evidence is less complete. It has been estimated that up to a third of all cats and dogs brought to veterinary surgeons for euthanasia, are destroyed because of behaviour problems. Substantial numbers are also abandoned or disowned by people for similar reasons (see §6.2.1), while those which are tolerated can drastically reduce the owner's quality of life.

In dogs, aggression directed either at the owner, the owner's family, or at strangers and other dogs, is the most common and serious form of behaviour problem. Male dogs tend to be more aggressive than bitches, although neutering (castration) will not always solve the problem. Over-excitability – hyperactivity and excessive barking – is also common, as is inappropriate urination or defecation in the home. Attachment-related problems, involving various manifestations of separation anxiety, are also a frequent source of difficulty when dogs are left alone. The scratching of household furniture and fabrics, urine spraying, and other inappropriate eliminative behaviour in the home, are the most common problems with cats.

Genetic predispositions are clearly involved in the development of many companion animal behaviour problems. Certain dog breeds, for example, such as guard dogs, have been deliberately selected for aggressiveness, while others may exhibit sudden outbursts of unprovoked aggression as a result of an inherited genetic defect (see §6.2.2). The animal's early experience is also crucial to the development of normal adult behaviour. Adverse psychological or social experience early in life, such as premature separation from the mother or litter-mates, or inadequate exposure to human company at the appropriate age, can also give rise to problems in otherwise normal, healthy animals. Inherited or acquired tendencies to respond abnormally or inappropriately can, in addition, be exacerbated by the manner in which the animal is treated by its owner (see §6.1.1).

The correct treatment of companion animal behaviour problems requires a reasonable knowledge of both animal and human psychology. Standard obedience training techniques are not always successful since they do not tackle the problem at its point of origin in the home, and tend to rely too heavily on physical discipline and punishment for misbehaviour. In general, successful treatment involves visiting the animal and its owner in the home environment and obtaining a clear picture of precisely the sorts of situation in which the problem arises. The animal's environment can then be modified so as to elicit more desirable behaviour, and the owner can be educated to alter his or her way of interacting with and rewarding the pet for correct or more appropriate responses. Physical treatment such as neutering may be beneficial in some cases, and a range of psychoactive drugs and hormone treatments can also be used in conjunction with behavioural retraining.

In some respects, the treatment of dog and cat behaviour problems resembles the treatment of emotional difficulties in children, in that the problem must be tackled within the context of the whole family, and not in isolation. Since the majority of problems arise because the owner unconsciously rewards the animal for misbehaving, successful treatment also depends largely on the owner's willingness or ability to modify their relationship with the pet, even when this may involve denying it affection or attention. Professional animal behaviour consultants report high rates of success in dealing with most companion animal behaviour problems, and there would appear to be scope for an expansion of this service in Britain. Because of their regular contact with pet-owners, veterinary surgeons are best placed to deal with such problems as they arise. Unfortunately, at present, few receive the necessary training to do so effectively. The inclusion of courses on animal behaviour and behaviour problems in the veterinary curriculum could greatly improve this situation (Mugford 1981; Voith and Borchelt 1982; Hart and Hart 1985; O'Farrell 1986).

6.2   PROBLEMS OF COMPANION ANIMAL WELFARE

6.2.1   *The abandonment and disposal of companion animals*

Although it is impossible to obtain accurate statistics on the total number of stray or abandoned companion animals in Britain, various estimates can be derived from the numbers taken in by individual animal welfare societies and charities. In addition to numerous individuals and small groups with similar aims, there are about 200 registered charities in Britain which run shelters or sanctuaries for homeless animals. Battersea, the largest dogs' home in the country, receives about 20 000 dogs and several hundred cats each year from an area of London with a human population of about 7 million. Applied nationally, this ratio would give an annual figure of roughly 150 000 stray or unwanted dogs, but this is undoubtedly an underestimate since several other animal rescue services in London also receive substantial numbers of animals. The major dogs' homes in Birmingham, Manchester, Edinburgh, and Glasgow have intakes which, as a ratio of the human population of these areas, would extrapolate to a national figure of between 300 000 and 400 000 lost, stray, or abandoned dogs each year. Previous estimates (see Studman 1983) have ranged from 200 000 to 1 million stray dogs, although the former figure was considered more accurate. About 80 per cent of dogs taken into shelters are classed as cross-bred with larger dogs in general predominating. Among the 20 per cent pure-bred, Alsatians (German shepherd dogs) are the most frequently sheltered. Their predominance is partly a reflection of the popularity of the breed, although the numbers taken in by shelters are still disproportionately high. The Cats Protection League, with about 140 branches nationwide, receives about 37 000 stray and unwanted cats each year, and several other large dogs' homes and shelters take in more than a thousand cats annually. The Wood Green Animal Shelter, with a clinic in London and two shelters near Cambridge, received 3500 dogs and 2700 cats in 1986, and another 700 animals belonging to other species ranging from horses to small rodents. The single species Donkey Sanctuary in Devon is currently sheltering nearly 3000 of these long-lived animals. Taking all these statistics into consideration, it is probable that at least 500 000 surplus companion animals are taken into care in Britain every year.

Animal shelters derive their intake from two major sources. Stray animals – principally dogs – account for substantial numbers, but it is not known what proportion of these are abandoned pets. At the Wood Green Animal Shelters, 20 per cent of cats and 12 per cent of dogs are received as strays or abandoned pets, but the proportions at other shelters may be higher. The Dogs Act 1906 gave statutory responsibility for the capture, custody, and disposal of stray dogs to the police, although it also allows members of the public to apprehend strays as long as they hand them over to the police. Since police stations are not always equipped to board stray dogs, animal shelters are often subcontracted to accommodate, find new homes for, or destroy such animals. Stray cats and other companion animals are not specifically covered by the law, and tend to be rounded up (and often destroyed) as and when they become a sufficient nuisance. The Abandonment of Animals Act 1960 makes it an offence for the owner or possessor of an animal to abandon it without good reason (whether permanently or not) in circumstances likely to cause unnecessary suffering.

Pet-owners who, for whatever reason, decide that they no longer wish to keep a pet are the other main source of animals received by shelters. For the past three years, the Wood Green Animal Shelter has collected reasons given by owners for parting with companion animals. The collated results, based on about 10 000 animals, indicate that, for 55 per cent of cats and 45 per cent of dogs, reasons were owner-related (allergies, arrival of new baby, divorce or separation, too many pets, unable to cope with or afford the animal, etc.). Animal-related problems (dirty, noisy, destructive, aggressive, etc.) were responsible for 5 per cent of cats and 17.5 per cent of dogs disowned, while miscellaneous (including the death or hospitalization of the owner) or unknown reasons accounted for 19 per cent of cats and 25 per cent of dogs. 'Too many pets' was the reason given for roughly a quarter of all admissions, and this was commonly the result of the indiscriminate breeding of cross-bred animals. The shelter is asked to find homes for the unwanted offspring and sometimes the mother as well.

The percentage of stray animals which are reclaimed by their owners ranges from 10 to 25 per cent depending on the shelter, although staff have learned to be wary of those falsely claiming lost dogs, especially if the animal belongs to a fighting or guarding breed. The proportions of animals which are found new homes is variable. Urban shelters tend to re-home from a quarter to a half of their intake, while some rural shelters, such as Wood Green, re-home 70 to 75 per cent of cats and dogs. The National Canine Defence League finds homes for 80 per cent of its dogs, and the Cats Protection League re-homes about 90 per cent of its cats. In some areas, cats are easier to re-home than dogs, but in others the reverse is the case. Only 3 out of 800 stray cats at Battersea were reclaimed in 1985, and none out of nearly 2000 at Glasgow. The policy of re-homing companion animals is sometimes criticized for being simply a procedure for recycling unwanted pets. Without some national scheme for registering and identifying animals, it is impossible to assess the extent to which this is true. In the meantime, many shelters attempt to reduce the problem by carefully matching each dog with its prospective new owner. Ideally the animal is observed by experienced staff before re-adoption, and the owner is also assessed by polite, but thorough, questioning. A few shelters also operate a system of follow-up visits to the animal's new home to check that it is adequately cared for. Such schemes are more feasible if the animal is not sold to, but rather adopted by, the new owner who then in law becomes its keeper. Pressures on time and staff at the busier shelters are often too great to permit follow-up schemes, although, generally speaking, shelters are willing to take back animals that prove unsatisfactory. The Donkey Sanctuary, a charity specifically devoted to the welfare of donkeys, provides shelter facilities and veterinary care for maltreated donkeys, and also inspects and monitors the welfare of donkeys at markets, donkey derby events, and seaside resorts. In 1986 the Sanctuary undertook 680 welfare visits to donkey owners to give advice. It also took in 307 animals of which 162 were subsequently found new owners.

By law, stray dogs must be held for a minimum of seven clear days, to allow the owner time to claim them, before being re-homed or otherwise disposed of.

Other companion animals are not protected to this extent, although most shelters will keep them for at least a week or two before considering more drastic options. Charities established for the protection and welfare of companion animals are, understandably, reluctant to have them destroyed but, at least in some cases, no feasible alternative exists. On veterinary advice, all shelters will terminate the lives of animals with serious injuries, debilities, or illnesses which are unlikely to recover. Unmanageable, aggressive, or excessively timid animals are also generally destroyed if it is apparent that they will never become satisfactory pets. Pressures on space at the busier shelters also necessitate the destruction of long-term inmates, if only because they would otherwise deprive another animal of a chance of life. The total number of pets destroyed varies enormously between shelters. In the smaller rural and semi-rural sanctuaries and shelters, few healthy animals are put down, but as many as two thirds are destroyed in some city shelters, particularly those that accept pets from owners for destruction, a practice which is justified on the grounds that the animal might otherwise be abandoned or put to death inexpertly or inhumanely by the owner.

All animal shelters fight a constant battle with epidemic disease, and some are at pains to isolate and vaccinate all incoming animals. The majority, however, have neither the space nor the funds to adopt this as routine procedure, and outbreaks of infectious disease, such as distemper, hepatitis, leptospirosis, parvovirus, and kennel cough in dogs, and cat flu and panleucopenia in cats, inevitably occur from time to time. Young and old animals are particularly susceptible, and disease undoubtedly accounts for a significant proportion of animals which die or are destroyed, particularly in the older, more overcrowded shelters. An increasing number of shelters also adopt a policy of neutering (see §6.2.3) as many cats and dogs as they can before re-adoption. When shortages of funds or manpower result in unneutered animals being re-homed, the shelter may ask the new keeper to sign an undertaking to have the animal neutered as soon as possible. Although some shelters will share the cost, a few owners object to having their animals neutered and may be supported in this by their local veterinary surgeon. All shelters offer some temporary accommodation for pets, although few provide boarding facilities for the animals of people going on holiday. Many, however, accommodate pets for owners who are temporarily incapacitated, in hospital, or remanded in custody, and close liaison often exists with local social services for this purpose. The Animal Boarding Establishments Act 1963 requires that premises used for boarding or housing dogs and cats on a commercial basis be licensed by their local authority. At present, animal shelters are not covered by the Act and no other regulations exist to ensure that shelters are providing their inmates with adequate care and facilities. While the majority of shelters do their best to fulfil their animals' needs, there is a case for arguing in favour of greater statutory controls on the proliferation of the smaller and less well-funded establishments where animals are sheltered.

6.2.2   Hereditary problems

Prior to the nineteenth century, the common varieties of companion animal were subjected to relatively little selective husbandry. Indeed, the majority of modern breeds arose primarily through long periods of genetical and geographical isolation, combined with the preferential treatment by people of individual animals displaying unusual or desirable physical or behavioural characteristics. Standards of animal care were rudimentary, and it is likely that any animal with inherited defects would either have died or been at a serious disadvantage compared with other, more robust individuals. Since about 1850, however, the selective breeding and showing of companion animals (see §4.3) has become a fashionable pursuit with many thousands of adherents, and the genetic effects of this hobby have not always been in the animals' best interests. Problems have arisen mainly for two reasons. Firstly, the original stock of animals used to establish a breed was often very small – sometimes only a handful of individuals – so the resulting gene pool was also limited. Secondly, in their efforts to standardize, consolidate, and enhance the characteristics of each breed, the breed societies selected small numbers of 'champions' whose genes then tended to predominate in subsequent generations. This, combined with generations of inbreeding, reduced the genetic variability of the breed still further, and encouraged the perpetuation and expression of unwanted or undesirable genetic defects. In a few breeds the effective gene pool is now so small and homogeneous, that it may be impossible to back-track and re-establish healthier genes in the population (Wolfensohn 1981). The dog has been the major victim of this process, although most domesticated animals exhibit comparable problems in less extreme or noticeable forms.

The number of different hereditary defects in dogs has been estimated at 75 (Malcolm Willis *in lit.*), although only about 20 breeds are seriously affected. Some of these disorders are largely the consequence of inbreeding or breeding from small numbers of genetically defective animals, while others are the result of breeders deliberately selecting for abnormal or accentuated physical characteristics. The former include such conditions as haemophilia, epilepsy, hereditary cataract, progressive retinal atrophy (PRA), and hip dysplasia. In general, most breeders and breed societies are keen to eliminate such problems, and organizations such as the British Veterinary Association and the Kennel Club operate schemes for detecting these defects early on so that animals bearing them are not used for breeding. Congenital defects (present at birth) are relatively easily detected and eliminated, but others are more difficult. PRA, for example, which may cause partial or total blindness in breeds such as poodles, Briards, collies, and Labradors, may not become apparent until well after the animal has reached breeding age.

Defects that arise as the direct or indirect result of deliberate selection pose a more intractable problem since many influential members of breed societies are passionately committed to maintaining the typical appearance of breeds as they stand, regardless of the animals' ultimate welfare. Typical examples of this type of problem include the foreshortened, wrinkled faces, and protruberant eyes of breeds such as pugs, bulldogs, and Pekingese; the drooping jowls and eyelids of bloodhounds and bassets, and the disproportionately short legs and long backs of bassets and dachshunds. Although some can be corrected by surgery, all of these defects can cause the animal serious discomfort. Ambiguous or inappropriate wording in the Breed Standard (the official written description of the breed) often contributes to the problem. The Breed Standard for the English bulldog, for instance, formerly stressed that the head of the ideal dog should be massive and large in proportion to overall size. As a result, breeders produced an animal with a cranium so large that some bitches have problems giving birth. Similarly, in their efforts to enhance the solemn facial expression of the bloodhound or St Bernard, breeders have created a condition known as *ectropion* in which the lower eyelid droops outwards exposing the delicate conjunctiva. The opposite condition, *entropion*, in which the eyelashes grow inwards is the result of selection for a diamond-shaped eye, which is considered desirable in breeds such as the chow chow. Recognizing the dangers, the Kennel Club has recently revised many of the more problematical Breed Standards in order to remove ambiguities and correct some of the existing faults. Unfortunately, no statutory laws exist to enforce such rules, and it is therefore up to the individual breeders, societies, and judges to respond to these changes in a responsible and humane way. The Council of Europe's Ad Hoc Committee of Experts for the Protection of Animals (Article 5, 1984) states that 'pet animals selected for breeding should have anatomical, physiological, and behavioural characteristics which are not likely to put at risk the health and welfare of either the offspring or the female parent.' Such pronouncements may form the basis for future EEC legislation, although it is difficult to envisage precisely how such laws would be enforced.

In addition to physical defects, pedigree dogs also exhibit behavioural disorders, some of which appear to have a strong genetic basis. A syndrome known as 'rage' or 'low threshold aggression' has been reported in English cocker spaniels which appears to fall into this category. It is characterized by violent and unpredictable outbursts of aggression, usually directed at the owner or the owner's family. Several other behaviour problems also occur more frequently than expected in certain breeds (Mugford 1984, 1985). For obvious reasons, inherited predispositions towards abnormal behaviour are more difficult to detect than physical defects and, at present, little is being done either to identify or eliminate them.

6.2.3 *Neutering and cosmetic mutilation*

Given the large surplus of companion animals abandoned or disowned each year, there are weighty practical and social reasons for arguing in favour of a policy of neutering animals which are not intended for breeding. Cats and dogs, in contrast to many livestock animals, must be anaesthetized for castration or spaying (Protection of Animals Acts 1911 to 1964) and, although these operations deprive the animal of normal reproductive behaviour, suffering is minimal, and it is extremely unlikely that the animal has any concept of the pleasures it might have enjoyed had it remained intact. Particularly in the case of male animals, castration also tends to reduce the animal's inclination to wander or stray when it may be involved in road accidents or fights with rival males. Castration also tends to make male animals less aggressive and territorial, although it has been reported that aggression is more common in spayed than intact bitches (Voith and Borchelt 1982). Neutered pets may show a tendency towards obesity, but this can usually be corrected through changes in the diet. There also appears to be little evidence to support the popular belief that female cats and dogs should be allowed to have a litter before spaying. The RSPCA, the Royal Collect of Veterinary Surgeons (RCVS), the British Veterinary Association (BVA), and the British Small Animal Veterinary Association (BSAVA) unanimously advocate a general policy of neutering companion animals.

Although emotive, the term 'mutilation' is the only accurate way to describe the current range of surgical procedures carried out on companion animals for non-therapeutic purposes. Those which cause greatest concern are procedures which are undertaken solely for cosmetic or fashion purposes, or for the convenience of individual owners. The RCVS recently established a Working Party to discuss the issue of animal mutilation and made the following recommendations: the surgical removal of normal functioning anal sacs from cats, dogs, or other species was considered unacceptable; the removal of claws was only acceptable if, in the opinion of a veterinary surgeon, injury to the animal was likely to occur if the claw(s) remained; cosmetic procedures on dogs' tails and ears, such as docking and cropping, were also unacceptable, as was the surgical devoicing or 'debarking' of dogs, except for therapeutic reasons. These opinions are also endorsed by the RSPCA, the BVA, and the BSAVA. The Council of Europe's Ad Hoc Comittee has also recently drafted a provision prohibiting all such procedures. Assuming the Convention is ratified by the United Kingdom, these practices will presumably be banned by law. Regrettably, by majority vote, the Kennel Club has condemned the EEC proposal to ban tail-docking.

Cosmetic procedures to correct the effects of genetic defects in companion animals pose a particular ethical problem for veterinary surgeons. While disapproving of the perpetuation of such defects on principle, veterinarians also have a responsibility to the animal to ameliorate its suffering. They are therefore placed in the unfortunate position of potentially aiding and abetting breeding practices that they consider unacceptable. This problem will only be resolved through the removal of such animals from the breeding population, and this will depend on a more responsible attitude among animal breeders and/or appropriate legislation.

6.2.4 *Other welfare problems*

Although all such activities are illegal, there seems to have been a recent resurgence of so-called 'cruel sports' involving dogs, particularly badger-baiting and dog-fighting. Both cause injury, death, and considerable suffering to the animals involved, although their adherents may justifiably claim that their sport is no more cruel than fox-hunting or hare-coursing, both of whch are legal. Pit bull terriers, often imported from the United States, are advertised openly for sale in the commercial press, and change hands for large sums of money. Considerable sums are also gambled on the outcomes of fights between these dogs. The practices are, however, difficult to eliminate entirely as they are conducted in extreme secrecy.

The breeding of dogs in Britain is controlled by the Breeding of Dogs Act 1973. Breeding establishments with two or more bitches on the premises must obtain a licence from their local authority, and be available for regular inspection by the authority's representative who, alas, need not be a veterinary surgeon. Establishments known as 'puppy farms' exploit a loophole in the 1973 Act by purchasing puppies from outside breeders and then rearing them *en masse* for subsequent sale. As no dogs are bred on the premises, these farms are not subject to inspection, and the conditions under which the animals are kept are often unsatisfactory. Pet-owners who obtain puppies from such sources also run the risk of acquiring an animal with serious behaviour problems as a result of its traumatic early experiences. The constant through-put of animals within these establishments also creates a fertile environment for disease infection. Under the 1973 Act, local authorities have no powers to inspect unlicensed premises where the commercial breeding of dogs is suspected but not proven, and some breeders also circumvent the regulations by farming bitches out in ones and twos to people who look after them on behalf of the breeder. In 1976 the Government's Interdepartmental Working Party on Dogs recommended changes in the Act to control such practices. So far, no changes have been made, despite the support of the various veterinary associations. Although local authorities do not appear to be aware of its potential, it is possible that puppy farms and other unlicensed premises could be inspected or closed down using the powers provided for in the Pet Animals Act 1951.

Since the last war there has been a substantial increase in the population of horses, ponies, and donkeys kept as companion animals. Regrettably, many of these pets are kept in poor conditions by people, often children, with little or no knowledge of how to look after them properly. As a result, many are diseased, malnourished, and afflicted with massive infestations of parasites. The British Veterinary Association and its specialist subdivision, the British Equine Veterinary Association, recently expressed concern about this problem, and have suggested ways of educating the public and encouraging more responsible ownership of such animals.

6.3   THE IMPACT OF TRADE IN EXOTIC PETS

Two main problems are raised by the use of wild and exotic species as companion animals or pets. The first concerns the possible impact of commercial trade on wild populations of the species involved, and the second concerns the welfare of the animals themselves. One study of the bird trade, for example, estimated that two of the world's largest exporters, India and Senegal, each collected and exported over 1 300 000 birds annually during the period 1970 to 1980 (Inskipp 1983). A more recent report by the Environmental Investigation Agency (EIA), however, indicates that Senegal may now be exporting as many as 10 million birds each year. This level of exploitation, particularly in combination with other factors such as habitat destruction, is likely to be seriously depleting populations of some species in the wild. It is also important to add to the equation the fact that, as species become less common in the wild, they tend to acquire rarity value to Western dealers and collectors, thus hastening their decline. There is little evidence that the pet trade alone has been responsible for the extinction of any species, but it has been responsible for drastic reductions in both the range and numbers of some animals. The virtual disappearance of Mediterranean tortoises from many parts of their former ranges is due almost exclusively to the depredations of the pet trade. Some of these reduced populations have shown signs of recovery since the trade was banned in 1984 (Luxmoore and Joseph 1986). In theory, current legislation ensures that permits for the commercial trade in threatened species are only granted when 'a scientific expert in the exporting country has advised that such export will not be detrimental to the survival of that species'. In practice, such rules are difficult to enforce.

On the welfare side, it is clear that many, if not most, wild animal pets do not adapt easily to captivity. Inskipp's (1983) study calculated that between 15 and 25 per cent of wild birds die, either during capture, transport, or quarantine, before reaching the retail market. The EIA report on Senegal, however, estimated that more than half of the birds captured die before export, and another 17 per cent during transport and quarantine. It is probable that substantial numbers also die soon after sale to purchasers who lack the knowledge and expertise to provide them with suitable living conditions. In the tropical marine fish trade it has been estimated that only about a third of those fish removed from the sea survive their first six months in captivity (Wood 1985). Compared with domestic species, most wild animals, especially those from tropical countries, have relatively specialized habitat and dietary needs. Yet no adequate legislation exists to ensure that a person who buys one will be aware of these needs or capable of providing for them. One of the most important factors leading to the eventual banning of the European tortoise trade was evidence indicating that 92 per cent of these animals died within their first three years of captivity (Luxmoore and Joseph 1986).

Resolution 1.6 of the Convention on International Trade in Endangered Species urged 'exporting countries to endeavour to restrict gradually the collection of wild animals for the pet trade, and that all contracting parties encourage the breeding of animals for this purpose with the object of eventually limiting the keeping of pets to those species which can be bred in captivity'. In the meantime, there would appear to be an urgent need for stronger controls on the import of exotic pets, and for closer monitoring of the trade in such animals, in order to ensure higher standards of care among both dealers and collectors.

6.4 PROBLEMS FOR THE COMMUNITY

6.4.1 *Pollution*

It has recently been estimated (see Baxter 1984*b*) that the canine population of Britain deposits about 4.5 million litres of urine and 1 million kilograms of faeces every day; some of it in streets, parks, playing fields, and other public areas where it is both aesthetically objectionable and often a considerable nuisance, and where it may pose a minor health hazard (see §6.4.2). The volume of excreta from cats has not been calculated, and most of it is deposited in private gardens or disposed of in cat litter. The fouling of public areas by dogs has, understandably, aroused considerable anti-pet feeling in recent years, and in many localities the problem has become a major issue provoking fierce hostility on both sides of the debate. Such feelings are unlikely to diminish until adequate methods of controlling the problem are found. Local by-laws make it an offence for people to allow their dogs to foul footpaths in some areas, but such rules are difficult to enforce, and many councils are apparently reluctant to prosecute (Studman 1983). Some councils have also imposed restrictions on dogs in parks, either banning them altogether, or cordoning them off into specific areas. Voluntary, public education 'scoop' campaigns are also underway in some boroughs, but it is somewhat doubtful whether social pressure alone will be sufficient to persuade many owners to tidy up after their pets. European cities, such as Toulouse in France, have experimented with specific toilet areas for dogs but, unfortunately, these have not been a success. A combination of public education, locally-administered 'scoop' laws (with fines imposed for fouling), and controlled access to public areas (particularly those where children play) would seem to be the most effective solution to the problem.

Noise constitutes the other major source of environmental pollution by companion animals, particularly from dogs and birds such as large parrots or macaws. Although the volume of sound produced by these animals is unlikely to damage human hearing, its intermittent and unpredictable character makes it particularly irritating and disturbing. Under civil law, individuals can take legal action against owners whose animals cause substantial discomfort or annoyance. Alternatively, local authorities can prosecute under the Control of Pollution Act 1974. Dog-owners may also resort to the drastic measure of having their pet surgically 'de-barked', although the veterinary profession is opposed to such procedures (see §6.2.3).

6.4.2   *Diseases and disease risks*

'Diseases and infections naturally transmitted between vertebrate animals and man' are referred to as zoonoses (WHO 1979). Such diseases can be transmitted directly to people through contact with animals, or they can be acquired indirectly from the environment. Contaminated food and water are the most important sources of zoonotic infection in the United Kingdom. Only a small proportion of zoonoses are acquired from companion animals and, of these, the most common are ringworm, toxoplasmosis, psittacosis, and pasteurella infection. Other zoonotic diseases, such as rabies, toxacariasis, and hydatid disease, have received considerable publicity in recent years, although most are comparatively rare (or absent, in the case or rabies) within the United Kingdom (Galbraith and Barrett 1986).

Ringworm   Ringworm is a fungal zoonosis which is caused primarily by one of two organisms: *Microsporum canis* acquired from dogs and cats, and *Trichophyton verrucosum* acquired from cattle. It is probably the commonest zoonotic disease in Britain, although frequencies of human infection are difficult to estimate. On average about 300 cases of *M. canis* infection are reported each year, but these figures probably grossly underestimate the actual incidence of the disease. A total figure of 9400 cases per year has been suggested, although this was derived from an elaborate extrapolation from limited data. Ringworm acquired from companion animals is not generally a serious condition, and it responds to treatment with a variety of antifungal drugs (Baxter and Leck 1984; Galbraith and Barrett 1986).

Toxoplasmosis   Toxoplasmosis is caused by the parasitic protozoan *Toxoplasma gondii*. It is widespread in animals, but cats are the definitive hosts and the most common source of infection in humans. People generally become infected by swallowing the parasite's oocysts (reproductive stage), either through handling infected cats or cat-litter, or by eating raw vegetables contaminated with soil containing cat faeces. The disease can also be acquired through eating raw or undercooked meat from infected animals, particularly sheep, goats, and pigs. In Britain, nearly one half of all adults over the age of 50 have been infected with toxoplasmosis at some time in their lives, and possess antibodies to the parasite in their blood. The vast majority, however, develop no symptoms. On average about 700 clinical cases of toxoplasmosis are reported each year, and there were 23 registered human deaths from the disease during the ten years between 1975 and 1984. Symptoms of toxoplasmosis include inflammation of the lymph glands, eye disease, and a glandular fever-like illness involving general malaise. The potential consequences during the early months of pregnancy are more serious; the parasite may invade the unborn fetus where it can cause death, hydrocephalus, and damage to the eyes and central nervous system. Most congenital infections are not fatal, and clinical symptoms only occur in 10 to 15 per cent of cases. Between 1976 and 1980, 62 per cent of reported toxoplasmosis cases involved eye disease, 27 per cent glandular illness, and only 4 per cent involved congenital symptoms. There is also no evidence that toxoplasmosis infection is on the increase, despite the rise in the cat population (Galbraith and Barrett 1986; Kirkwood 1987).

Cats generally acquire the disease through eating infected rodents, and 60 per cent or more of cats possess antibodies to the parasite. The animals, however, are only infectious for a few weeks while they are excreting oocysts. The danger to human health is therefore small and can be minimized, particularly for pregnant women, by wearing gloves when gardening, washing hands before eating (especially after handling raw meat), and avoiding contact with cat litter. A variety of antibiotics have been used in the successful treatment of the disease.

Psittacosis Psittacosis or ornithosis is caused by the virus-like organism, *Chlamydia psittaci*, strains of which cause disease and often occur without symptoms in a wide variety of mammals and birds. Mammalian strains appear to be of low pathogenicity to humans. People generally acquire the disease by inhaling the dust from the droppings or feathers of infected birds, or from air-borne material in poultry (especially duck) processing plants. The disease can also be spread from person-to-person, and it is possible that some strains have become adapted to man as a primary host. Between 1975 and 1984, 2561 cases of human infection were reported in England and Wales, and 11 fatalities. Of those infected, 20 per cent were said to have had contact with birds, and 9 per cent with parrots. Symptoms of psittacosis in humans are often described as flu-like, and generally manifest themselves as atypical pneumonia or non-specific fever. Treatment with the antibiotic tetracycline is generally effective in controlling the disease in both humans and animals.

Psittacosis appears to be one of the few zoonotic diseases that is on the increase in Britain. Incidences of human infection have more than doubled since 1975, although the proportion of bird-associated infections has remained the same. The reason for this increase is unknown (Galbraith and Barrett 1986; Kirkwood 1987).

Pasteurella infection Pasteurella is a widespread bacterial infection in animals. Two species, *Pasteurella multocida* and *P. pneumotropica*, commonly inhabit the mouths of dogs and cats and comprise the main source of infection in humans. The disease is transmitted to people through bites and scratches. The usual result is a local infection around the wound, although respiratory disease, meningitis, and septicaemia may also occur. 2937 cases of human infection were reported in England and Wales between 1975 and 1984, of which 2750 were caused by *P. multocida*. Animal bites, especially from dogs, were responsible for 80 per cent of these cases. Most infections were localized, 247 involved respiratory illness, 60 produced septicaemia, and only 9 involved meningitis. There were no reported fatalities from the disease. Although these statistics probably underestimate the incidence of Pasteurella infection (see Baxter and Leck 1984), there is little evidence of any recent increase in the disease, despite the growth of the dog and cat population (Galbraith and Barrett 1986).

Toxocariasis or visceral larva migrans   Human toxocariasis derives primarily from infection by the larval stages of two species of common roundworm, *Toxocara canis* and *T. cati*. The worms' primary hosts are dogs and cats, respectively, and the former represent the main source of human infection. The disease was first recognized in humans during the 1950s when the larval stages of *T. canis* were identified in tissue samples from children suffering from diseases of the liver, lungs, and retina. Because of its resemblance to retinoblastoma (a particularly malignant cancer), the eyes of some children suffering from toxocariasis were mistakenly enucleated. Humans acquire the disease by ingesting the parasite's eggs, either from contaminated soil or via contact with infected animals. The larvae then migrate from the alimentary canal and through the tissue of the liver, the lymphatic system, the lungs and, occasionally, the eye and brain where they form granular cysts. Children in the age group three to five are most usually affected. This age effect has been attributed to their fondness for dogs, their use of parks and playgrounds where dogs have defecated, and their habit of playing in and often ingesting soil.

In the dog, the parasite has a complex life cycle. Larvae are mobilized from the tissues (usually the muscles) of pregnant bitches during the final stages of pregnancy. They then migrate through the placental wall and infect the liver of the unborn fetus. These larval migrations are probably triggered by hormonal changes in the pregnant bitch. In the newborn puppy, the larvae complete their development by migrating from the liver to the lungs, and thence to the pharynx where they are swallowed to develop to maturity in the puppy's intestine. Adult worms are produced 20 to 40 days after birth. Larvae lose this ability to migrate once the puppy is beyond 3 months of age. After this, newly acquired larvae distribute themselves in the animal's body tissues where they remain dormant unless reactivated by pregnancy and lactation. Dogs, like humans, may also acquire *Toxocara* by ingesting the parasite's eggs, or by eating the dormant larval stages which also occur in the tissues of rodents.

This life cycle emphasizes puppies and pregnant or nursing bitches as important sources of human infection and environmental contamination. At this time the animals may develop substantial adult worm burdens and pass large numbers of eggs in their faeces, leading to heavy contamination of soil, etc., in the immediate vicinity of the home. Public areas where dogs are walked – parks, playgrounds, sidewalks, and commons may also be contaminated with parasite eggs, although surveys of soil from public parks indicate considerable variation in this respect. Only 2 per cent of soil samples from some parks were contaminated, while from others it was as high as 24 per cent.

Despite the levels of environmental contamination, toxocariasis infection in humans is rare. Immunodiagnostic tests have established that about 2.5 per cent of the general population possess antibodies to the parasite, indicating that they have been infected at some time in the past. In the vast majority of cases, no symptoms were manifest. Rates of subclinical infection appear to be higher among persons, such as dog-breeders and exhibitors, who have extended contact with dogs. Within such groups, positive tests for the presence of *Toxocara* antibodies increase in proportion to the length of time the person has engaged in dog-breeding and the number of bitches whelped each year. Positive antibody tests also seem to be somewhat higher than the general average in people suffering from uveitis, liver enlargement, and asthma (10 per cent, 29 per cent, and 17 per cent, respectively), suggesting that infection by the parasite may have been involved in a minority of cases. Between 1975 and 1984, only 107 clinical toxocariasis infections were reported in England and Wales, an average of about ten cases per year.

Effective control of *T. canis* is now possible. Puppies and nursing bitches should be regularly examined for infection, and a number of anti-worm drugs can be administered to eliminate the larval stages of the parasite. Formerly, the dormant (somatic) stage of *Toxocara* was untreatable, but recent experimental trials with various benzimidazole compounds have proved effective against the parasite in adult dogs. Regular treatment of puppies and breeding bitches can therefore drastically reduce the number of larvae and eggs available for infection or environmental contamination. Efforts must also be made to educate the dog-owning public to reduce the amount of faecal contamination of public recreation areas, especially those where young children play. Children should also be discouraged from allowing nursing bitches, in particular, to lick their hands and faces. Although the burden of responsibility for *Toxocara* control rests with dog-owners, the veterinary profession has a crucial role to play as a source of advice, education, and treatment (Galbraith and Barrett 1986; Kirkwood 1987).

Hydatid disease   Hydatid disease or hydatidosis is caused by the larval (hydatid) stage of the dog tapeworm, *Echinococcus granulosus*. In Britain, the sheepdog is the definitive host, and it acquires the infection by eating hydatid cysts in raw sheep offal and meat. The adult worms develop in the dog's alimentary canal where they lay eggs which are then excreted in the host's faeces. Sheep become infected with the parasite by ingesting the eggs while grazing. Humans (usually farmers and their families) also acquire the disease by accidentally ingesting the parasite's eggs, either after handling affected dogs or via faecal contamination of food. In man, the parasite migrates from the gut into the liver, lungs, kidneys, brain, and other tissues where it forms cysts. The cysts develop slowly and clinical symptoms may not become apparent for several years, by which time the effects may be serious. Treatment is by surgical removal of the cysts.

103 human cases of hydatidosis were reported in England and Wales between 1975 and 1984, and 43 registered deaths. These figures, however, probably under-represent the true incidence of the disease. Fortunately, the risks to the general public are very small because the disease has an extremely localized distribution in this country. At present hydatid disease is endemic to parts of mid-Wales and the Scottish islands where, in a small population, the incidence is reputed to be the highest in western Europe. Effective control measures include treating affected dogs with appropriate anti-worm compounds, and educating farmers not to allow their dogs to feed or scavenge from sheep carcasses (Galbraith and Barrett 1986; Kirkwood 1987).

Rabies   Rabies is the most greatly feared of all zoonotic infections. The disease is caused by a virus and is transmitted to humans primarily through animal bites. Affected animals secrete the virus in their saliva. The virus cannot penetrate intact skin, although infection can occur through any open wound or abrasion. In man, the virus ascends the nerves to the brain, salivary glands, and main nerve trunks where it produces a variety of neurological symptoms. As the disease progresses, generalized paralysis is followed almost invariably by death. In animals, such as dogs, two clinical symptoms are observed. In the paralytic or 'dumb' form of the disease the animal stands or sits with its jaws hanging open, and is unable to swallow or close its mouth. In the 'furious' form the animal behaves in an erratic, anxious manner, and will attack fiercely virtually anyone or anything it encounters.

Rabies has not been endemic to Britain since 1922. Rigorous controls over the importation of wild and domestic animals under the Rabies Act 1974 (now contained within the Animal Health Act 1981), and compulsory six months quarantine for most imported mammals, has so far succeeded in preventing the reintroduction of rabies into Britain, despite the current epidemic in mainland Europe (Woodrow 1975; Bekaert 1982). Effective vaccines against rabies are now available for dogs and cats, and are widely used on the Continent. It is debatable, however, whether the present system of import controls and compulsory quarantine should be relaxed in the case of vaccinated animals.

Other zoonotic infections   Although a great many other diseases and infections can, in theory, be acquired from companion animals, only a few pose any significant health risk in this country. Of these, the bacteria *Salmonella* and *Campylobacter* are probably the most important, although contaminated food is the usual source of infection. Both cause enteritis in humans. Cat scratch fever, DF-2, and *Yersinia* can also be acquired from pets of various kinds, but the incidence is extremely rare. Occasional cases of human dermatitis have also been attributed to animal fleas and mange mites. It should also be mentioned that several zoonotic diseases can produce acute or fatal symptoms in immuno-compromised (AIDS) individuals.

Other health risks   Many people become sensitized to the scurf, fur, and feathers of animals, and to animal mites. Allergic symptoms usually develop during childhood and generally consist of hay-fever, rashes, asthma, or diarrhoea when the person is in contact with animals, especially dogs and cats. An allergic condition known as bird breeders' or bird fanciers' lung also occurs in people who keep captive birds, such as pigeons. The condition results from inhaling organic material in dust, and causes the formation of granular tissue in the lungs (Kirkwood 1987).

6.4.3   *Accidents, injuries, and damage*

Animal bites   For Britain as a whole, no reliable statistics exist on the incidence of companion animals biting people. Estimates, however, have been calculated from studies at individual hospitals, particularly in the north of England during the 1970s. According to such figures, animal bites and stings account for between 1.2 and 3 per cent of attendances at hospital casualty units, and the majority involve bites from dogs. Extrapolations for the country as a whole have produced frequencies of between 99 000 and 200 000 bites per year, of which roughly 90 per cent consist of minor or superficial injuries requiring no further hospital attendance. In a small proportion of cases, bites from dogs and cats may result in bacterial infections (see §6.4.2). Among the general population, children in the age group 5 to 19 are at greatest risk, and in all age groups, males are more likely to be bitten than females. Dog bites occur at higher frequencies during the summer months, at weekends, and on public holidays, and most victims are bitten either by their own dogs, or at least by dogs known to them. Roughly half of all biting incidents occur in or near the owner's home. North American statistics suggest that about 65 per cent of reported bites take place while the animal is being played with, fed, teased, abused, or separated from another dog, and 35 per cent were classified as unprovoked by the victim. Male dogs, large dogs, and dogs less than a year old appear to be the main offenders (Studman 1983; Baxter 1984*a*).

Certain sectors of the population, such as delivery workers, face a particular danger from dog bites. The Union of Communication Workers recently circulated a letter to MPs expressing the anxiety of Britain's 120 000 postmen and women concerning this hazard. Within the last ten years, dog attacks on postal workers have apparently increased by more than a third from 3992 cases in 1976 to 77 to 5560 in 1986. The Post Office estimates that such incidents cost more than £250 000 annually in sick pay. In one incident in Gloucester, a postwoman had her ear torn off and suffered multiple bites to her hand, face, and legs when attacked by three German shepherd dogs (*Daily Telegraph*, 20 August 1986). Postal workers have also been obliged recently to declare parts of the London borough of Eltham a 'no go area' because of the ferocity of dog attacks. Family pets are responsible for the majority of such incidents.

Judging from the limited information available, dog bites arise from two major sources. Most occur while people are playing or interacting with their own or familiar pets, and result either from the animal's general excitability and exuberance, or from rough handling. Because they tend to play with and tease family pets, children are at greater risk, although the bites involved are not usually serious and frequently unintentional. Canine territorial aggression appears to be the other important source of biting incidents, and the consequences tend to be more serious, particularly in view of the recent increase in the popularity of large and potentially dangerous guarding breeds (see §4.1.1). Under the Dogs Act 1871, magistrates can order a dangerous dog to be kept under proper control. On failure to do so, the court can order the animal's destruction. There is apparently no legal basis for the widely-held belief that every dog is entitled to one free bite. Any attack by a dog renders its owner liable, although animals with a history of such attacks are more likely to be ordered destroyed than one which suffered a single aberration. In addition, the Guard Dogs Act 1975 requires that, unless properly secured, these dogs shall not be used unless they are under someone's immediate control. Premises using guarding dogs must also post warning messages to this effect.

Accidents   Free-roaming companion animals are prone to dashing into or across roads where they may cause traffic accidents. Not all such accidents are reported to the police and, in some cases, drivers may blame 'fictional' dogs or cats to conceal their own incompetence. Nevertheless, available statistics allow estimates to be made of the scale of the problem, at least as far as dogs are concerned.

Figures published by the Royal Society for the Prevention of Accidents indicated that 75 000 dogs were involved in road accidents in 1951. 61 per cent were killed outright, 35 per cent were injured, and 4 per cent escaped unharmed. 3000 human casualties resulted, of which 600 were seriously injured and 23 were killed. More recent figures are somewhat less alarming. Between 1971 and 1981, for example, the number of road accidents involving dogs (and some form of injury to people) remained fairly constant at around 1600 per year, or 0.6 per cent of the annual total of 250 000 accidents. During the three years, 1978, 1979, and 1981 (for which figures are available), an average of 17 human fatalities were recorded each year, or 0.3 per cent of the total human death toll on the roads. Approximately 82 per cent of dog-associated accidents occurred in built-up areas (Studman 1983). Regional calculations generally confirm these findings and emphasize that the vast majority of such accidents involve no injuries to people. A survey conducted in Greater Manchester found that, of all accidents involving injury to people in which dogs were implicated, 0.9 per cent were fatal, 22.8 per cent involved serious injury, and 76.4 per cent caused slight or minor injuries. Strays, feral animals, latch-key, and unleashed dogs are apparently the greatest offenders, since only 0.3 per cent of recorded accidents involved dogs on leads (Baxter 1984*a*). Baxter (1984*a*) estimated the annual financial cost of dog-associated accidents at £40 million, of which 85 per cent represented damage to property. The figure, however, is largely speculative and difficult to either confirm or refute. No statistics at all are available on cat-associated traffic accidents, but it must be assumed that wandering cats also contribute to a small proportion of damages, injuries, and deaths on the roads. Under Section 31 of the Road Traffic Act 1972 it is an offence for a person to cause or permit a dog to be on a designated road without being on a lead. A designated road is a road that has been specified as such by the local authority. Since the procedures involved in designating a road are lengthy and expensive, most authorities are reluctant to enforce such rules except in a minority of cases.

The British Horse Society has recently expressed its concern over the number of road accidents involving horses and ponies, and their riders. They estimate that as many as eight such accidents occur each day in Britain. As a first step towards reducing this hazard, the Society has published a booklet, *Riding and Roadcraft*, and a road safety training video.

In addition to posing a minor hazard on the roads, companion animals also cause a number of accidents in the home. The miscreants, however, tend to be house pets rather than strays or free-roaming animals, and the victims are generally either the animal's owner or a member of the family. Hospital figures for 1976 indicate that 0.54 per cent of all home accidents (not including bites) are caused by, or associated with, dogs; a total of 325 accidents per year. Again, information on cat-caused accidents is not available. The vast majority of such accidents involve only minor injuries (Baxter 1984*a*).

6.4.4 *Damage to livestock and other animals*

While accidents involving dogs are primarily an urban phenomenon, dog attacks on livestock tend, for obvious reasons, to occur in rural or semi-rural areas. Unfortunately, the Ministry of Agriculture discontinued the collection of data on dogs attacking and worrying livestock in 1979, so no recent figures are available. Information from the previous four years, however, indicated that about 10 000 livestock animals were killed or injured by dogs each year. Attacks on sheep – more than half of which were fatal – accounted for roughly 75 per cent of incidents, while attacks on poultry represented about 20 per cent of the total. Cattle, pigs, goats, domestic rabbits, horses, or ponies were involved in about 5 per cent of cases. Assuming these figures still hold true, the annual cost in compensation to farmers must be in the region of £250 000. Although stray dogs are responsible for some attacks, inadequately controlled family pets are often to blame (Studman 1983). The Wildlife and Countryside Act 1981 makes it an offence for a dog to be at large in a field or enclosure where there are sheep, unless it is on a lead or otherwise under close control. This carries a maximum fine of £200. Section 9 of the Animals Act 1971 also allows farmers to kill dogs worrying livestock, if no other reasonable means of control is effective, and if the owner is not in the vicinity. The owner may also be liable to pay compensation to the farmer to make good any financial loss he or she incurs.

Dogs also attack and injure or kill cats, sometimes with the owner's connivance or encouragement. It is, however, impossible to assess the extent of this problem.

Worldwide, feral companion animals, especially dogs and cats, have been responsible for considerable damage to wild animal populations, and probably some extinctions. In Britain, naturalized or feral pets are less of a problem, although pet rabbits released by their owners on at least one offshore island may now be threatening the survival of burrow-nesting seabirds, such as puffins. Wandering dogs and, to a lesser extent, cats also pose a serious danger to seabirds and waders which nest on beaches. Budgerigars and ring-necked parakeets have established small feral populations in some localities (Kirkwood 1987), but their impact on native species is unknown. It has also been suggested that interbreeding with feral or semi-feral domestic cats may be threatening the genetic integrity of the native wildcat in Scotland. Stray and free-roaming dogs also pose a significant risk to wild deer populations.

6.4.5   *The disposal of dead companion animals*

An increasing problem for veterinary surgeons practising in urban areas is the disposal of the carcasses of small animals (chiefly dogs and cats) that have been destroyed by euthanasia, died during treatment, or brought to the veterinary surgeon for disposal by the owner. The cost of incineration facilities is beyond the means of most veterinary practices and, in any case, it is likely that few local authorities would grant permission for the installation of such incinerators in urban or suburban areas.

While it is the responsibility of local authorities to provide collection of commercial waste, including waste from veterinary premises (including animal carcasses and other animal tissues), such collection is frequently unsatisfactory or does not occur. Some reports also indicate that animal carcasses have been left to decompose on municipal rubbish tips.

Alternative arrangements for the disposal of animal carcasses may be made with private companies. Although the majority of such companies provide an efficient and acceptable service, a substantial handling fee is often charged which is passed on to the client by the veterinary surgeon. Storage facilities, such as deep-freezes, may also be required between collections, adding to the expenditure for disposal. In addition, the public image of private disposal companies has been tarnished by reports of the carcasses of pets being processed for fat or fertilizer, and their skins being sold for fur or leather goods.

The Department of the Environment has recently drafted a new Control of Pollution (Collection and Disposal of Waste) Regulation 1987 in which waste from veterinary premises would be regarded as commercial waste, and it would be the duty of the local authority, if requested, to arrange its collection and disposal. There is a pressing need to regularize local authority responsibility for the disposal of small animal carcasses.

6.4.6 Competition for food

As indicated earlier in this study (see §4.2.1), British pet-owners purchase in excess of a million tonnes of prepared food for their dogs and cats each year. Some authorities view this level of consumption of edible material by non-utilitarian animals as wasteful, particularly considering the present degree of human malnutrition in many parts of the world (see for example Mellanby 1975). Although the equation of human food versus animal food appears superficially compelling, in reality the amount of direct competition for edible resources between people and pets is very small. Pet foods account for only 4 per cent of the total UK food market, and the Pet Food Manufacturer's Association, which represents over 90 per cent of the industry in Britain, has a policy of acquiring raw materials that are unsuitable for, or surplus to, human consumption. Animal protein – meat and fish – is obtained almost entirely as offal and trimmings from the meat or fish processing industry. If it was not purchased for pet food, much of this material would be wasted and the rest of the carcass would be proportionately more expensive to human consumers. The availability of prepared pet foods has, in addition, reduced the demand for fresh meat and fish to feed companion animals. Most of the cereals used in pet foods are also either surplus or considered unsuitable for milling (PFMA Profile, 1987).

Even assuming that companion animals did not exist, the redistribution of such raw materials to developing countries would pose considerable practical, economic, and sociopolitical difficulties, not the least of which would be the acceptability (or lack of it) of such foods to people of other cultures and religious persuasions. Admittedly, pet-ownership in the West does not benefit the mass of humanity, but this is equally true of the vast majority of Western leisure activities. Singling out pet-owners for restriction or penalty would therefore be difficult to justify on ethical grounds.

6.5 SUMMARY

Virtually all human activities entail some degree of risk or harm, and pet-keeping is no exception. Among the problems created by pet-ownership, those that reduce the welfare of the animals, and those which generate danger, inconvenience, or expense for other members of the community are, under-standably, the ones which cause greatest concern. In both cases, most problems are created by people obtaining pets for the wrong reasons and then failing to give them adequate supervision and care. This kind of careless and irresponsible attitude to pet-ownership not only affects the welfare and survival of companion animals, but can also cause pollution, disease, accidents, and other problems for society. Such attitudes are often based on ignorance, and public education could do much to minimize the harm they cause. On the welfare side, animal breeders, especially dog breeders, are vulnerable to criticism for perpetuating harmful genetic defects and for encouraging the mutilation of companion animals for the sake of fashion. Those who trade in or keep exotic species as pets must also be blamed for causing unnecessary suffering to animals during capture and transport, and for depleting wild populations of the species involved. It is also clear, from the numbers which are abandoned, disowned, or destroyed every year, that far too many companion animals are being produced, and that a major effort should be made to reduce the effective size of the breeding population through neutering.

As far as the interests of society are concerned, the greatest hazards are caused by dogs, chiefly strays and those which are allowed to roam around unsupervised. Apart from causing serious and sometimes fatal traffic accidents, these animals are responsible for pollution and periodic attacks on livestock. Over-aggressive and badly disciplined pet dogs are also an increasing threat, particularly to children and delivery workers. In this respect, the growing popularity of large guarding breeds is especially worrying, since, in the wrong hands, these animals can become dangerous or even lethal. Public education, systems of licensing and registration, and heavy penalties for the owners of offending animals would seem to be the only solution to such problems. Despite the considerable publicity it has received, the danger to human health from companion animal-borne diseases is slight. Nevertheless, when combined with justifiable aesthetic objections to the pollution of public areas by dogs, the problem should be seriously addressed and, as far as possible, minimized. Again, public education and certain restrictions on dogs in recreation areas would seem advisable. In this, as in most matters pertaining to companion animals, veterinary surgeons have a special role to play as advisors and educators. It would therefore be beneficial if such topics received greater coverage in the veterinary curriculum.

7 An ethical comment

It would be easy to moralize upon the narrative parts of this study, and to dignify the process with the name of 'ethics'. But if the narrative is well written, the ethical issues will present themselves, and readers will recognize them as such. The recognition may reveal itself in no more than a feeling of unease: 'if this be so', the reader may say to himself, 'ought it to be so?' Are we right to do it, or to encourage it, or to let it happen? The facts do not by themselves define an ethical problem. Still less can they solve it. We recognize an ethical problem arising from the facts when, deliberately or, more commonly, without conscious effort, we judge them against some received assumptions about right and wrong. Where these assumptions come from is an academic question not to be pursued here. The fact is that they are part of our common culture, our inherited morality, the corporate possession of a society or people – though not, in the matter of animals, of *every* society or people.

Not everyone in our society shares these assumptions. But they are of sufficient currency to generate unease in the minds of ordinary, moderately reflective and sensitive people when they are infringed. Conversely, some believe that these moral assumptions are not stringent enough; that they embody shameful compromises from which we should be recalled. Such provocation to examine our axioms is valuable provided that it is exercised lawfully and reasonably. We are constantly under pressure to be lax; to allow causes to go by default. Such pressure comes from within – to take the easier course of action – or from without, when commercial or other interests are at stake. It is the function of ethics to relate the narrative, the facts of the case, to the moral assumptions. Ethics is, in this context, the exercise of moral reasoning: the attempt, by reasoned appeal, to enable people to work out the right course of action for themselves, and for their corporate life in society, in relation to the facts before them.

The facts, as narrated in this study, have been ordered by human minds, and this order is the product of assumptions implicit in those minds. They have set out what they believe to be true according to authorities they assume to be reliable. But even so, the ordering and emphasis have been governed, to some extent, by prior moral assumptions. The evidence, for instance, concerning species threatened by over-exploitation for the pet trade would not be so collected and presented were not the threat of species extinction seen as a moral issue claiming attention. Similarly, the facts concerning cosmetic mutilation or dysgenic breeding would not be organized around these subject headings unless they were perceived as moral issues.

The present commentary, therefore, is not an extended series of tut-tuts; an icing or veneer on the story told. It is rather an analysis of the moral claims raised by the story; an enquiry into *why* these moral claims arise. The aim of the enquiry is to take readers into the reasoning of it, so that they may themselves emerge with more understanding of their own attitudes to companion animals, and some reasoned conviction, perhaps, on which to stand.

7.1   RIGHTS AND DUTIES

Why do moral issues arise in the study of companion animals? They arise, as do most moral issues, out of a tension between interests. History is relatively clear on this. The human species has exploited animals – whether for food, for labour, for adornment, for sport, or for companionship – specifically to serve human interests. The fact becomes morally problematical once it is recognized that animals also have interests. The first moral issue, therefore, is the reconciliation between the potentially conflicting interests of people and their animal companions.

Human interest is not only individual but also corporate. A multitude of personal decisions, taken to serve personal interests, can have widely ranging social consequences, amounting to, or threatening, a corporate social interest. So the moral issues concerning companion animals are not soluble only in terms of the two sentient creatures concerned; the human and the animal in companionship. They spill over into the social domain; they raise questions of social policy. They prompt questions about the effects of pet-keeping on corporate life organized into civic communities of various sorts. And, our conscience being what it is, they also prompt questions about the immediate and ultimate interests of the animals involved.

But why can we speak of 'animal interests'? It is because we recognize in animals sensitivities similar to our own. The degree of sensitivity may vary, but it is fair to say that in the species commonly kept as pets the nervous system is sufficiently developed for us to postulate a sense of pain and distress, on the one hand, and of well-being, if not of pleasure, on the other. It would follow that the accepted moral assumptions which lead us to recognize and respect the human interest in avoiding pain and distress, or enjoying well-being and pleasure, must extend to the recognition and respect for comparable interests in companion animals. One may venture this extension without anthropomorphism: the imputation of human qualities to animals. What is imputed here is a range of sensory and biological affinities varying widely in degree.

It is one of the moral assumptions of our society (and of many others) that a duty exists to protect the interests of animals, thereby setting limits on what may be done to them in order to satisfy human needs and desires. It is not necessary to invest animals with rights in order to assert and enforce that duty. The duty arises from the intellectual and moral perceptions which are a product of human nature. We can recognize duties without attributing rights. Historians, scientists, and journalists, for example, may feel obliged to penetrate the truth of things and to present it truthfully, without assuming any 'right' invested in anyone to receive it. The truth itself exerts its own moral claim. There are duties attaching to kinship, friendship, neighbourliness, and common vulnerability which are unmatched by rights. The unborn child has no rights – until born alive – as the law understands the term. Yet the law imposes duties for the child's protection. So with companion animals or, indeed, animals used in medical experiments or sport. They are a concern of ethics because, in their sensitivity and vulnerability, they press moral claims upon us analogous to, though not coterminous with, those presented by human kind.

Similarly with society. The body corporate has claims upon its members individually, and we have duties towards the society in which we live. Some of these claims are specified and enforced by law: we can speak of 'statutory duties'. Local authorities can also specify such claims in by-laws. But it would not be for the common good, or for the good of individuals, if we limited our concept of duty to what the State or the local authority has chosen to enforce. The human conscience has a social dimension. It recognizes duties corporate as well as personal.

Posterity has no rights. It would be foolish, for example, to posit a 'right' in a Mediterranean tortoise to continue to exist; or a 'right' in a rainforest not to be cut down; or a 'right' in Epstein's Madonna in Cavendish Square to be preserved for posterity. Yet we acknowledge in ourselves a duty to protect and conserve these things. The language of 'rights', fascinating as it may be in the discourse of philosophy, exploited as it may be in liberationist polemic, is not a necessary tool in the calm and determined duty of protecting the interests of other species.

7.2   SPECIFIC ISSUES

The companion animal – sentient, aware, and vulnerable – is the meeting point of several concentrations of interests. Those of its owner; of its owner's neighbour, who may either take pleasure in its existence or annoyance at its barking, or fouling of the pavement; of the local community which must contain the potential conflict of interests within its jurisdiction; of the ancillary occupations and trades – breeders, suppliers of pet foods, veterinary surgeons – and, of course, of the animal itself and the species which it embodies.

7.2.1   *The trade in exotic animals*

Respect for the animal will urge that it and its kind be not trivialized. The very organic miracle which makes tropical fish or Mediterranean tortoises objects of fascination morally forbids – that is, forbids by intrinsic moral appeal – the casual removal of large numbers of specimens from their natural habitat for personal satisfaction or commercial gain. This practice is even more reprehensible when many, or most, will die prematurely, either in capture, transit, or in their new, uncongenial habitat.

7.2.2   *Irresponsible pet-ownership*

The same consideration raises serious questions about the acquisition and keeping of pets as temporary playthings or objects of amusement. Such casual attitudes not only imperil the animal, but also their owners, by giving them a false notion of their place and power in the natural order. The potential impact on children is of particular concern. A child who learns to regard animals as toys misses valuable educational opportunities. To induct a child into the wondrous understanding of an animal, thereby to teach him sensitive care, is to induct him into a first understanding of his own affinity with other species; to bring into awareness his own sentience, his capacity for relationship, and his duty to respect and conserve. Even the mentally handicapped child or adult, who may not possess an intellectual awareness of such things, may nevertheless gain emotionally from the warmth of a relationship with a companion animal.

7.2.3   *To kill, or not to kill?*

At the other pole, respect for the animal can itself be problematical. In reaction, no doubt, to man's historic arrogance in disposing of animal life at his own arbitrary will, there are groups who scruple at taking any animal's life. So, donkey sanctuaries exist for donkeys whose lives have become sancrosanct. Some animal lovers are shocked when they learn of animal shelters operating, necessarily, a policy of destroying animals when the numbers sheltered reach the limit of possibility. One may admit sympathy with such scruple without allowing it much ethical cogency. Death is natural to all living creatures, universal and necessary in the biological order. The moral questions attend the manner and circumstances of the death, and the motive for it – a subject too wide to be pursued here.

A special case may occur for a veterinary surgeon whose professional duty may be, on occasions, to kill. The animal is his patient; its owner his client. Contractually, he is engaged to serve his client's interest in the animal. But professionally he is obliged to consider his patient's interest, sensitive and vulnerable as it is. Sometimes, therefore, he must insist on putting down a suffering animal which the owner would rather keep alive. At other times he may be under pressure to put down a healthy animal which its owner insists on repudiating. But what would be the veterinarian's duty if some 'lover' of animals directed in his will the destruction at his death of the menagerie he had gathered around him in life? Would he be bound professionally to perpetrate that destruction? Or would it be his professional duty to refuse to do so in order to repudiate, in the name of his profession, so distorted a view of human dominion over other living creatures? How would a Court adjudicate between the executors, with their duty to carry out the testator's wish, and the veterinary surgeon claiming a liberty and duty to refuse? One would suggest that the Court could declare the testamentary direction void because it was contrary to the public interest; namely the upholding of a relationship between man and animal from which arbitrary tyranny is excluded – and this to protect humanity in man. Such a judgement would but give judicial expression to an assumption implicit in the narrative chapters of this study.

7.2.4 Neutering

The neutering of pets is sometimes held to be an improper violation of the animal's nature, in depriving it of its natural power to procreate and have its young. In simple truth, the fertility of domestic animals poses the same problem as that met in human populations by contraception and other means of fertility control. Over-production of pets creates considerable problems for society, and inevitably results in distress and suffering for many thousands of surplus companion animals each year. Animals are not equipped to take voluntary measures of population control. It is therefore within the responsibility of their human owners to take those measures for them, humanely, and with the least impairment of their natural ways of life.

7.2.5 Dysgenic breeding and cosmetic mutilation

The deliberate breeding of dogs and other pets to accentuate dysgenic characters, such as foreshortened faces, bulging eyes, drooping eyelids, or disproportionately short legs and long backs, stands on a different footing. It is done for the satisfaction of 'fanciers', and to win prizes or admiration at shows. It can be adverse to the well-being of the animals. It reflects a distortion of the proper relation of man to beast, commonly described in terms of responsible stewardship. It certainly merits social discouragement by voluntary bodies such as pet clubs, breeders' associations, and by the veterinary profession. But only when inflicted suffering is proved could it be brought under the sanction of the criminal law. The same argument holds for the cosmetic mutilation of companion animals, although proof of suffering through the performance of unnecessary surgical procedures is clearly easier to obtain.

7.2.6 The dog licence

As far as the juridicial status of pet-keeping is concerned, it cannot be assumed as a right. Rather it should be regarded as a liberty, sanctioned by long continuance and warranted – as this study shows – by mutual benefit when properly exercised. (To recognize mutual benefit when it exists is not to ignore evident instances of harm.) Yet the liberty, like others in society, may be regulated by positive law, and sometimes must be. One instrument of regulation, now under political discussion, is the dog licence. The dog licence is now practically obsolete in Great Britain, and legislation to abolish it is currently progressing through Parliament. The fee is 37 pence *per annum*, a sum which, even if every dog-owner paid it, would raise less revenue than it costs to collect. In Northern Ireland the fee was recently raised to £5 *per annum*.

Strictly speaking, a licence represents formal permission to perform an action which would be illegal, or at least illicit, without a licence. Licences are commonly granted on proof of capacity and competence to perform the act in question, and conditions are attached, for a breach of which the licence may be withdrawn. A clear example is the licence to drive a motor vehicle. The applicant must be of a certain age; he must pass a driving test; his licence may be endorsed or withdrawn in case of offence against the Road Traffic Acts or, when through age or infirmity, he becomes no longer fit to drive. The motor vehicle itself is not licenced but taxed. The purpose of the tax is to raise revenue, ostensibly for road building, maintenance, and signs. The cost is substantial, and it is an offence to drive a vehicle untaxed, or not to display a disc certifying that the tax has been paid.

Should dog-keeping be subject to licence, or to tax, or to neither? Any such impost is, to some extent, an anomaly since other pets are not subject to it. Justification, therefore, must depend either on the need to recompense the public purse for costs incurred, or on the necessity to control the activity. A straight tax on dogs would provide revenue from which local authorities could provide services, such as dog-wardens, in the public interest. This, with appropriate by-laws, could raise the standard of hygiene in the streets and public areas. The dog would carry a small tax disc on its collar, and it could be an offence to keep a dog untaxed – an enactment which might result in an initial increase in the numbers of homeless and ownerless animals. A licence, on the other hand, could be granted for the keeping of a dog, and upon some *prima facie* evidence of competence to do so. If the dog were neglected or ill-used, the licence could be withdrawn. It could also be withdrawn if the dog were inadequately controlled, or caused a public nuisance or danger. Postmen, and other delivery workers report attacks, and the increasing ownership of large, potentially dangerous breeds, such as Dobermanns, German shepherds, and Rottweilers, as domestic guard dogs increases the hazard. Domestic guard dogs are not subject to legislation as are guard dogs for commercial premises, and a differential licence fee might be an effective means of controlling them. The licence fee, and the conditions of grant, should be stringent enough to bring home to potential dog-owners the seriousness of the undertaking. Exemptions could be granted for special categories, such as guide dogs, dogs used in shepherding or farming, or others kept for specified supportive or protective purposes. The licence fee would also yield an annual revenue.

Judging from the evidence and concern displayed in this study, there would appear to be social advantage in imposing a dog licence at a fee consistent with the seriousness of the undertaking, and high enough to cover the cost of collection. Any extra revenue could be used by local authorities to provide relevant services. The evidence from Northern Ireland does not support the view that a £5 licence fee would seriously disadvantage or deter responsible dog-keepers, or lead to an increase in the numbers of abandoned animals. It might, on the contrary, discourage casual and irresponsible ownership. Such a licence, it is understood, would have the support of the veterinary profession and the majority of bodies concerned with animal welfare and with the environment. It could be politically unpopular, to the extent that parties in opposition might try to make political capital out of reviling the government which proposed it. Politics was at one time considered to be a branch of ethics, both concerned with justice. In the relationship of man and animals, justice and compassion cannot stand far apart.

7.3 CONCLUSION

It is evident from this study that the keeping of companion animals is a widespread and entrenched feature of life in modern Britain. It satisfies human interests; it is not ordinarily contrary to the social or public interest and, in the absence of abuse, it is not in itself contrary to animal interests. The report has indicated where abuse can and does occur. Such a widespread social habit must have a recognized place in public policy. It would be consistent with public policy in general to leave the government of the practice, so far as possible, to voluntary control exercised on the basis of an ethics accepted by people at large and by related bodies, voluntary and professional. Where this proves insufficient as protection for serious interests – those of the animal, or of children in danger from domestic pets, or of neighbours or passers-by, or of the local community – then legislation, national or local, is called for. One major purpose of this study has been to help an informed public to deliberate and to decide where the balance of control should lie.

8 Recommendations

The present study has described the current status of companion animals and their ownership in the United Kingdom, and has outlined some of the benefits and problems arising from this unique and important animal–human relationship. Because it is largely beneficial and rewarding to both participants, relatively few aspects of this relationship entail serious conflicts of interest between people and animals. Most of the problems which do exist could be substantially reduced or eliminated by appropriately directed research, public re-education and, where necessary, improved statutory controls. The Working Party therefore proposed the following recommendations.

8.1 MANIFESTATION AND RECOGNITION OF SENTIENCE

Man is generally well-intentioned towards companion animals. Most people would not wish consciously to cause pain or stress to their lives and, indeed, will try to increase their experience of pleasure. We have no direct access to the consciousness of animals so we tend to use our conscience as a guide to action. We are aware of obvious sentient signals but may conclude erroneously that in the absence of such signals there is no sentience. There is need for study and research on the manifestations and recognition of sentience in animals; the factors that modify these, and their signalling of responses to humans.

8.2 PSYCHOSOCIAL BENEFITS OF COMPANION ANIMALS

Scientific understanding of the potential psychosocial benefits of pet-ownership is extremely limited. There is considerable scope for more research in this area, and on finding methods of applying the results in the therapeutic use of animals in hospitals, hospices, nursing homes, sheltered housing, prisons, and in the community at large.

8.3 ABANDONMENT OF COMPANION ANIMALS

Research into the social, emotional, and/or economic factors underlying the abandonment, destruction, and inadequate care and supervision of companion animals would be fruitful. Abnormal or inappropriate behaviour patterns in companion animals often contribute to the breakdown of owner–pet relationships; detailed studies of the development of such behaviour problems, together with attempts to identify and eliminate predisposing genetic factors would be of great value.

8.4 EDUCATION OF COMPANION ANIMAL OWNERS

Many of the problems created by companion animals arise through owners' ignorance of their needs. Intensified programmes of public education, disseminated via schools, television, radio, and the press, are therefore needed. Much of this educational material should relate to health since good health, to a large extent, is equated with good welfare. The messages can be simple, with unequivocal information provided on such matters as the importance of regular vaccination and de-worming of dogs and cats, the consequences of pollution of public recreation areas, and the dangers associated with unsupervised, free-roaming dogs. It is important to persuade the public to restrict, by neutering or other means, the breeding of cats and dogs, both in the interests of the community and of the animals themselves.

8.5 EDUCATION OF VETERINARIANS

Because of their special relationship with the companion animal-owning public, veterinarians are in a unique position to influence owners' attitudes and behaviour. It would therefore be of benefit if the problems associated with human–companion animal relationships received greater coverage in the veterinary curriculum: in particular, areas such as companion animal behaviour and behavioural problems; euthanasia and client grief; and ethical issues concerning animals should receive emphasis.

8.6 HEREDITARY PROBLEMS

An increasing number of hereditary problems are being recognized in companion animals, especially dogs. Many of these are the consequences of inbreeding or breeding from genetically defective animals. Some are the result of deliberate selection for abnormal or unnaturally accentuated physical characteristics for fad or fancy. Collectively, such breeding practices are a distortion of the generally assumed responsibility man has for companion animals. Greater efforts should be made to discourage breeding for physical malformations, particularly those requiring corrective surgery.

The Kennel Club and the breed societies should make more use of their dominant role in this area, and it is recommended that stricter criteria for entry and judgement at shows, etc., be introduced so as to disqualify animals with physical defects specifically encouraged by fashion and which compromise the health and welfare of the animals involved.

8.7   COSMETIC MUTILATIONS

Surgical alteration of a tissue or structure for non-therapeutic purposes is regarded as a mutilation and, in some instances, is prohibited by law. Certain alterations to dogs are also contrary to the rules of the Kennel Club. Nevertheless, some mutilations (for example, the docking of dogs' tails or the removal of cats' claws) are still practised for purely cosmetic purposes or for the convenience of owners, and it is recommended that these be prohibited by law.

8.8   LEGISLATION

Owing largely to historical factors, current legislation relating to companion animals and their owners is dispersed across a wide range of different Parliamentary Acts. As a result, the legal status of companion animals is particularly confusing and incoherent. Judging from the current rate of change of public opinion regarding companion animals, many of these laws are likely to require amendment in the near future and, to expedite such changes, it would be beneficial to legislators, the courts and society as a whole if all existing and future legislation were to be consolidated within a single Companion Animals Act.

8.9   INSPECTION OF PREMISES

Despite the recommendations of the Government's Interdepartmental Working Party on Dogs (1976), The Breeding of Dogs Act 1973 still contains a loophole which is exploited by unscrupulous dog-breeders and dealers (for example, puppy farms). It is recommended that the law be amended at the earliest possible opportunity to encompass such establishments. Although present regulations require that pet shops, dog breeding establishments, and animal boarding kennels be inspected by a representative of the local authority, the officer in question need not be, and commonly is not, a veterinarian. We recommend that future legislation ensures that all such inspections be carried out by a qualified veterinary surgeon. Consideration should also be given to extending the powers of the Animal Boarding Establishments Act 1963 to include animal shelters.

8.10   STRAY AND UNSUPERVISED ANIMALS

If public education proves inadequate as a means of encouraging owners not to allow dogs to stray or roam unsupervised, we recommend changes in the law so as to enforce 'leash laws' on all major roads. Fines for persistent offenders might also be considered.

8.11   EXOTIC ANIMALS

The list of species which, at present, cannot be imported for commercial purposes should be enlarged to include both those which are known to be rare or under threat in the wild, and those which, for a variety of reasons, do not generally flourish in captivity. In the past, a special case was made for Mediterranean tortoises, and there would appear to be an urgent need either to modify existing legislation or to create new laws to protect a much wider range of species. Since the welfare of these animals is frequently at risk through public ignorance, pet traders and dealers should be under a statutory obligation to provide adequate written information on the care of exotic animals to all prospective purchasers.

8.12   THE DOG LICENCE

The Working Party does not support the Government's decision to abolish the dog licence. Dogs undoubtedly create greater problems for society and, in purely numerical terms, their welfare is more at risk than most other kinds of companion animals. We therefore recommend a national dog licence with a fee set at between £5 and £10. The revenue collected from such a licence should be used exclusively for the benefit of dogs and their owners and to reduce the undesirable affects of dog-ownership on the community as a whole. Specifically, we are in favour of a locally administered dog warden service. Such a service would take responsibility for the collection, care, and disposal of stray or abandoned animals out of the hands of the police, as well as providing advice and education to the dog-owning public. We further suggest that guide dogs and other dogs for disabled or physically impaired persons be exempt from such licensing arrangements. Consideration should also be given to increasing the licence fee for some of the larger and more aggressive guard dog breeds, and to reducing it for neutered animals.

The Working Party could find no evidence that the proposed licence would result in a substantial increase in the numbers of abandoned dogs. On the other hand, its existence might help to deter the casual or irresponsible dog-owner. A licence would also have the advantage over a straight tax on dogs in that it could be withdrawn from owners who proved incapable of looking after a dog properly. To be effective, such a licence would need to be linked with a system of identifying licensed animals.

Appendix

(UK Legislation referred to in the text)

The Dogs Act 1871–1906 (sections 6.2.1 and 6.4.3)
The Protection of Animals Act 1911–1964 (section 6.2.3)
The Pet Animals Act 1951 (sections 4.2.4 and 6.2.4)
The Abandonment of Animals Act 1960 (section 6.2.1)
The Animal Boarding Establishments Act 1963 (sections 4.2.3 and 6.2.1)
The Riding Establishments Acts 1964 and 1970 (section 4.3.3)
The Animals Act 1971 (section 6.4.4)
The Road Traffic Act 1972 (section 6.4.3)
The Breeding of Dogs Act 1973 (sections 4.3.1 and 6.2.4)
The Control of Pollution Act 1974 (section 6.4.1)
The Guard Dogs Act 1975 (section 6.4.3)
The Dangerous Wild Animals Act 1976 (section 4.1.7)
The Endangered Species (Import and Export) Act 1976 (section 4.1.7)
The Animal Health Act 1981 (section 6.4.2)
The Wildlife and Countryside Act 1981 (section 6.4.4)

For further information on laws relating to companion animals see: *Legislation Affecting the Veterinary Profession in the United Kingdom* (The Royal College of Veterinary Surgeons, London, 1984).

Bibliography

BOOKS AND ARTICLES

Baxter, D. N. (1984a) The deleterious effects of dogs on human health: 1. dog-associated injuries. *Community Medicine* **6**, 29–36.

Baxter, D. N. (1984b). The deleterious effects of dogs on human health: 3. miscellaneous problems and a control programme. *Community Medicine* **6**, 198–203.

Baxter, D. N. and Leck, I. (1984). The deleterious effects of dogs on human health: 2. Canine zoonoses. *Community Medicine* **6**, 185–97.

Bekaert, D. A. (1982). *Handbook of diseases transmitted from dogs and cats to man*. California Veterinary Medical Association, Moraga, CA.

Bennett, T. and Wright, R. (1984). What the burglar saw. *New Society*, 2 February 1984.

Bowd, A. D. (1984). Fears and understanding of animals in middle childhood. *Journal of Genetic Psychology* **145**, 143–4.

Broad, S. (1986). Imports of psittacines into the UK 1981–1984. *Traffic Bulletin* **8**, (3), 36–9.

Bustad, L. K. (1980). *Animals, aging and the aged*. University of Minnesota Press, Minneapolis.

Bustad, L. K. and Hines, L. M. (1983). Placement of animals with the elderly: benefits and strategies. In *New perspectives on our lives with companion animals* (ed A. H. Katcher and A. M. Beck). University of Pennsylvania Press, Philadelphia.

Corson, S. A. and O'Leary Corson, E. (1980). Pet animals as nonverbal communication mediators in psychotherapy in institutional settings. In *Ethology and nonverbal communication in mental health* (ed S. A. Corson and E. O'Leary Corson). Pergamon Press, Oxford.

Delafield, G. (1976). *The effects of guide-dog training on some aspects of adjustment in blind people*. University of Nottingham, PhD Thesis.

DePauw, K. P. (1984). Therapeutic horseback riding in Europe and North America. In *The pet connection* (ed R. K. Anderson, B. L. Hart, and L. A. Hart) pp. 141–53,. Center to Study Human–Animal Relationships and Environments (CENSHARE), University of Minnesota, Minneapolis.

Dismuke, R. P. (1984). Rehabilitative horseback riding for children with language disorders. In *The pet connection* (ed R. K. Anderson, B. L. Hart, and L. A. Hart) pp. 131–40,. CENSHARE, University of Minnesota, Minneapolis.

76 Companion Animals in Society

Edney, A. T. B. (1984). Bigger and better. *Pedigree Digest* **11**,(3), 3.

Franti, C. E., Kraus, T. F., Borhani, N. O., Johnson, S. L., and Tucker, S. D. (1980). Pet ownership in rural northern California (El Dorado County). *Journal of the American Veterinary Medical Association* **176**, 143–9

Friedman, E., Katcher, A. H., Lynch, J. J., and Thomas, S. A. (1980). Animal companions and one-year survival of patients after discharge from a coronary care unit. *Public Health Reports* **95**, 307–12.

Friedmann, E., Katcher, A. H., Thomas, S. A., Lynch, J. J., and Messent, P. R. (1983). Interaction and blood pressure: influence of animal companions. *Journal of Nervous and Mental Disease* **171**, 461–5.

Friedman, E., Katcher, A. H., and Berger, B. (1984). Pet-ownership and psychological status. In *The pet connection* (ed R. K. Anderson, B. L. Hart, and L. A. Hart), pp. 300–8. CENSHARE, University of Minnesota, Minneapolis.

Galbraith, N. S. and Barrett, N. J. (1986). Emerging zoonoses. *Journal of Small Animal Practice* **27**, 621–46.

Guttman, G., Predovic, M., and Zemanek, M. (1985). The influence of pet ownership on non-verbal communication and social competence in children. In *The human–pet relationship*, pp. 58–63. IEMT, Vienna.

Hart, B. L. and Hart, L. A. (1985). *Canine and feline behavioural therapy*. Lea and Febiger, Philadelphia.

Hines, L. M. (1983). Pets in prisons: a new partnership. *California Veterinarians* **5**, 7–17.

Hutton, J. S. (1983). Animal abuse as a diagnostic tool in social work. In *New perspectives on our lives with companion animals* (ed A. H. Katcher and A. M. Beck), pp 444–7. University of Pennsylvania Press, Philadelphia.

Inskipp, T. (1983). The Indian bird trade. *Traffic Bulletin* **5**,(3–4), 26–46.

Katcher, A. H. (1981). Interaction between people and their pets: form and function. In *Interrelations between people and pets* (ed. B. Fogle), pp. 41–67. Charles C. Thomas, Springfield, Ill.

Katcher, A. H., Segal, H., and Beck, A. M. (1984). Contemplation of an aquarium for the reduction of anxiety. In *The pet connection* (eds R. K. Anderson, B. L. Hart, and L. A. Hart), pp. 171–8. CENSHARE, University of Minnesota, Minneapolis.

Kirkwood, J. K. (1987). Animals at home – pets as pests: a review. *Journal of the Royal Society of Medicine* **80**, 97–100.

Lago, D. J., Connell, C. M., and Knight, B. (1985). The effects of animal companionship on older people living at home. In *The human–pet relationship*, pp. 34–46. Institute for Interdisciplinary Research on the Human–Pet Relationship (IEMT), Vienna.

Lee, D. R. (1983). Pet therapy – helping patients through troubled times. *California Veterinarian* **5**, 24–5 and 40.

Levinson, B. M. (1969). *Pet-oriented child psychotherapy*. Charles C. Thomas, Springfield, Ill.

vinson, B. M. (1972). *Pets and human development.* Charles C. Thomas, Springfield, Ill.

ckwood, R. (1983). The influence of animals on social perception. In *New perspectives on our lives with companion animals* (ed A. H. Katcher and A. M. Beck), pp. 64–71. University of Pennsylvania Press, Philadelphia.

xmoore, R. and Joseph, J. (1986) UK trade in tortoises. *Traffic Bulletin* **8**(3), 46–7.

ellanby, K. (1975) *Can Britain feed itself?* Merlin Press, London.

essent, P. R. (1983). Social facilitation of contact with other people by pet dogs. In *New perspectives on our lives with companion animals* (ed A. H. Katcher and A. M. Beck), pp. 37–46. University of Pennsylvania Press, Philadelphia.

essent, P. R. and Horsfield, S. (1985). Pet population and the pet-owner bond. In *The human–pet relationship*, pp. 9–17. IEMT, Vienna.

igford, R. A. (1981). Problem dogs and problem owners: the behaviour therapist as an adjunct to veterinary practice. In *Interrelations between people and pets* (ed. B. Fogle), pp. 295–317. Charles C. Thomas, Springfield, Ill.

igford, R. A. (1984). Aggressive behaviour in the English Cocker Spaniel. In *The veterinary annual*, 24th Issue, pp. 310–14. John C. Wright, Bristol.

igford, R. A. (1985). Attachment vs. dominance: alternative views of the man–dog relationship. In *The human–pet relationship*, pp. 157–65. IEMT, Vienna.

igford, R. A. and M'Comisky, J. G. (1975). Some recent work on the psychotherapeutic value of cage birds with elderly people. In *Pet animals and society* (ed. R. S. Anderson), pp. 54–65. Baillière Tindall, London.

Farrell, V. (1986). *Manual of Canine Behaviour.* British Small Animal Veterinary Association, Cheltenham.

sen, G., Anderson, R. K., Quigley, J. S., and Beahl, N. (1983). Pet-facilitated therapy: a study of the use of animals in health care facilities in Minnesota. In *New perspectives on our lives with companion animals* (ed A. H. Katcher and A. M. Beck), pp. 431–5. University of Pennsylvania Press, Philadelphia.

ce, S., Brown, L., and Caldwell, H. S. (1973). Animals and psychotherapy: a survey. *Journal of Community Psychology* **1**, 323–6.

lmon, P. W. and Salmon, I. M. (1982). *A dog in residence: a companion animal study undertaken at the Caulfield geriatric hospital.* Joint Advisory Committee on Pets in Society (JACOPIS), Melbourne, Australia.

lmon, P. W. and Salmon, I. M. (1983). Who owns who? Psychological research into the human–pet bond in Australia. In *New perspectives on our lives with companion animals* (ed A. H. Katcher and A. M. Beck), pp. 244–65. University of Pennsylvania Press, Philadelphia.

rpell, J. A. (1981). Childhood pets and their influence on adults' attitudes. *Psychological Reports* **49**, 651–4.

rpell, J. A. (1983). The personality of the dog and its influence on the pet–owner bond. In *New perspectives on our lives with companion animals* (ed A. H. Katcher and A. M. Beck), pp. 57–63. University of Pennsylvania Press, Philadelphia.

Serpell, J. A. (1986). *In the company of animals.* Basil Blackwell, Oxford.

Sherick, I. (1981). The significance of pets for children; illustrated by a latency age girl's use of pets in her analysis. *Psychoanalytical Studies of the Child* **36**, 193–215.

Studman, C. J. (1983). *The dog today: the problems and the solutions.* Universities Federation for Animal Welfare, Potters Bar, Herts.

Thomas, K. (1983). *Man and the natural world: changing attitudes in England 1500–1800.* Allen Lane, London.

Tuan, Yi-Fu (1984). *Dominance and affection: the making of pets.* Yale University Press, New Haven.

Voith, V. and Borchelt, P. (1982). Diagnosis and treatment of dominance aggression in dogs. *Veterinary Clinics of North America/Small Animal Practice* **12**, 655–64.

Whyte, A. M. (1987). Pets in prisons. *Pedigree Digest* **13**,(3), 10–11.

Winnicott, D. W. (1953). Transitional objects and transitional phenomena. *International Journal of Psychoanalysis* **24**, 88–97.

Wolfenson, S. (1981) The things we do to dogs. *New Scientist*, 14 May 1981.

Wood, E. (1985). *Exploitation of coral reef fishes for the aquarium trade.* Marine Conservation Society, Hereford.

Woodrow, C. E. (1975). The supply and distribution of pet animals. In *Pet animals and society*, pp. 113–19. Baillière Tindall, London.

Woods, S. M. (1965). Psychotherapy and the patient's pet. *Current Psychiatric Therapy* **5**, 119–21.

Zahn-Waxler, C., Hollenbeck, B., and Radke-Yarrow, M. (1985). The origins of empathy and altruism. In *Advances in animal welfare science 1984–85* (ed M. W. Fox and L. D. Mickley). Humane Society of the United States, Washington, DC.

Zee, A. (1983). Guide dogs and their owners: assistance and friendship. In *New perspectives on our lives with companion animals* (ed A. H. Katcher and A. M. Beck), pp. 472–83. University of Pennsylvania Press, Philadelphia.

REPORTS AND OTHER PUBLICATIONS

Report of the Interdepartmental Working Party on Dogs (1976). HMSO, London.

Parasitic Zoonoses (1979). Technical Report Series 637, World Health Organization, Geneva.

The Keeping of Companion Animals in Local Authority Housing Developments (1981). Joint Advisory Committee on Pets in Society (JACOPIS), London.

Draft Provision of the Ad Hoc Committee of Experts for the Protection of Animals (1984). Council of Europe, Strasbourg.

PFMA Profile (1987). Pet Food Manufacturer's Association, London.